BOA
EDITIONS
LIMITED

Breaking the Alabaster Jar:
Conversations with Li-Young Lee

The printing of this book was made possible, in part,
by a generous donation from the Mary S. Mulligan Charitable Trust,
and by the generous support of Jane Schuster, whose gift honors
the heart-intelligence of BOA poets Anthony Piccione and
Li-Young Lee.

Books by Li-Young Lee

Rose. Rochester, NY: BOA Editions, 1986.

The City in Which I Love You. Rochester, NY: BOA Editions, 1990.

The Winged Seed. New York: Simon & Schuster, 1995.

Book of My Nights. Rochester, NY: BOA Editions, 2001.

Breaking the Alabaster Jar: Conversations with Li-Young Lee

Edited by Earl G. Ingersoll

American Reader Series, No. 7

BOA Editions, Ltd. ⟩⟩⟩⟩ Rochester, NY ⟩⟩⟩⟩ 2006

Publications by BOA Editions, Ltd.—a not-for-profit corporation under section 501 (c) (3) of the United States Internal Revenue Code—are made possible with the assistance of grants from the Literature Program of the New York State Council on the Arts; the Literature Program of the National Endowment for the Arts; County of Monroe, NY; the Lannan Foundation for support of the Lannan Translation Selection Series; Sonia Raiziss Giop Charitable Foundation; Mary S. Mulligan Charitable Trust; Rochester Area Community Foundation; Arts & Cultural Council for Greater Rochester; Steeple-Jack Fund; Elizabeth F. Cheney Foundation; Chadwick-Loher Foundation in honor of Charles Simic and Ray Gonzalez; Chesonis Family Foundation; Ames-Amzalak Memorial Trust in memory of Henry Ames, Semon Amzalak and Dan Amzalak; and contributions from many individuals nationwide.

For Information about permission to reuse any material from this book please contact The Permissions Company at www.permissionscompany.com or e-mail permdude@eclipse.net

See Colophon on page 192 for special individual acknowledgments.

Cover Design: Lisa Mauro
Cover Photo: Andrew Downes
Back Cover Artwork: "Symbiology" by Li-Lin Lee, photo courtesy of Walsh Gallery
Interior Design and Composition: Richard Foerster
Manufacturing: McNaughton & Gunn, Lithographers
BOA Logo: Mirko

Library of Congress Cataloging-in-Publication Data

Lee, Li-Young, 1957–
Breaking the alabaster jar : conversations with Li-Young Lee / edited by Earl G. Ingersoll.— 1st ed.
    p. cm. – (BOA Editions American readers series ; no. 7)
  ISBN 1-929918–82–8 (pbk. : alk. paper)
  1. Lee, Li-Young, 1957—Interviews. 2. Poets, American–20th century–Interviews. 3. Poetry—Authorship. I. Ingersoll, Earl G., 1938–
II. Title. III. American reader series ; v. 7.

PS3562.E35438Z46 2006
811'.54–dc22
2006004124

NATIONAL
ENDOWMENT
FOR THE ARTS

BOA Editions, Ltd.
250 North Goodman Street, Suite 306
Rochester, NY 14607
www.boaeditions.org
A. Poulin, Jr., Founder (1938-1996)

State of the Arts

NYSCA

Contents

Breaking the Alabaster Jar

Introduction

One place to begin this collection of interviews with Li-Young Lee is the inevitable question he is asked by interviewers: "Where are you from?" Occasionally when he is in a playful mood, he answers, "Chicago," deflecting the interviewer's obvious efforts to engage the poet in a discussion of his identity as an Asian American. If compelled to confront questions of his ethnicity, he stresses very forcefully that although he was born in Indonesia he rejects any effort to label him Indonesian, since Indonesia under Sukarno imprisoned and tortured his father shortly after Lee was born. Lee spent his early childhood there and has fond memories of an Indonesian nanny whom he attempted unsuccessfully to locate when he returned to Indonesia as a young adult. As he strongly emphasizes, however, his parents were ethnic Chinese, who felt forced to emigrate from China as they had struggled to find their place in their homeland after it became Communist in 1948. When Lee visited China it was not a Homeland for him. One of the palatial homes his mother's family lived in when she was a child had been converted into a hospital, and the family's lands had become public parks. During the Cultural Revolution the bones of his mother's family were dug up and scattered about. Even Lee's brother who died in China after the family emigrated appears to have been buried in a mass grave. And yet Lee obviously continues to have ties to Chinese culture; for example, he speaks to his mother in Chinese, her only language, not in English, his second language after Mandarin Chinese. On the other hand, his first poem was in English and he has not written in Chinese. Because those who know Lee's poems, but especially the memoir *The Winged Seed*, are familiar with his comments on his family background and early life, an effort has been made to reduce those elements in the conversations to follow in order to emphasize the provocative remarks Lee makes about the writing of his poems and about his sense of the writer's craft.

As he tells interviewers, Lee is well aware that excessive emphasis on his life and especially on his ethnicity can direct attention away from the poems themselves. Clearly the identity of Asian-American poet has the potential of ghettoizing those who might be drawn in by the possibilities of exploiting their ethnicity to advance in a culture intent on marketing writers through their ethnicities. Even more, however, as he indicates again and again, Lee knows how indebted he is to American poets, older poets such as Walt Whitman and Emily Dickinson, but also more recent poets such as Philip Levine and Gerald Stern. He might well identify himself as Asian-American to the census taker at his door; however, it is as an American poet that he would see himself first and foremost. At the same time, he might be a little hesitant to use that high-powered term *poet* because he still feels, as recently as the Fox interview, that he has to evolve toward those "great poets" he so admires: "In order to write like Emily Dickinson, for instance, I have to change." As he indicates more than once, when he sits down at the kitchen table at night to write poems, he is not likely to think to himself, Here I am, an Asian American setting out to compose an Asian-American poem. Indeed, in the Cooper and Yu interview he voices this concern with ethnicity very bluntly: "When they introduce Philip Levine to do a reading, they don't say, 'Here's the Jewish-American poet, Philip Levine.' They just say 'the American poet.' When they introduce me, they say, 'He's the Chinese-American poet.'" Some of these issues take a less somber course in the conversations. When his sons asked about their ethnicity and he explained that he is ethnic Chinese and their mother Donna is Italian-American, they responded that they were "half-Chinese" and "half-regular." Often his interviewers seem impelled to get him to confirm an identity as a spokesman for the Asian diaspora; they soon discover, however, that he refuses the role of spokesman for anyone or anything—except perhaps the supreme worth of art. In seeing himself as an American, he also addresses issues of homelessness to which many Americans can respond, especially as he admits to a sense of displacement, a sense that his home is someplace else.

As these conversations demonstrate, Lee was influenced by the Chinese culture of his parents and by the Christian culture to which his father introduced the family when he left China (where he was one of Mao Tse-tung's physicians), to become a highly successful evangelist preacher. Lee recalls hearing his parents recite poems from the repertoire of hundreds that each was expected to memorize as part of their classical Chinese education. Perhaps more importantly, he recalls his father reading from the King James translation of the Bible. It is small wonder, then, that Lee as a poet would continually testify to the sanctity of words and the inherent spirituality of the poet's profession. Readers of these conversations soon become convinced that poetry is a highly serious endeavor for Lee, given his own very real sense of *vocation*. Again and again, Lee talks about the practice of art in the context of the word *yoga*, whose Sanskrit origins denote a "link," as in the Latin word *religio*, also meaning "link," or "connection." "All art to me is yogic practice," he says, because art yokes our true natures to a total consciousness that we might identify as God. "Total presence," he adds, "is the grail" that poets aspire to, even though they are aware of the odds against finding the Grail.

Voice is crucial, he argues, for the poem is "a score for the human voice." Such a voice that seems "almost omniscient" is at the same time the voice of the poet's "nobody-hood," a term Lee generates out of his hero Emily Dickinson's lines, "I'm Nobody! Who are you?" This is a voice beyond language, like a voice we hear from another room: individual words may be indiscernible, but the voice is hardly without meaning. This is a voice striving to find a "language to inflect silence," a deeper silence, like the silence one hears after a bell stops pealing. Paradoxically, Lee as a poet has his reservations about language, calling it at one point an inconvenience, perhaps because for him the primary function of language is cognition, or knowing, with communication as a distant secondary function. A poem, he speculates, may be the silence we hear after we finish reading the poem's words. Although the term makes him somewhat uneasy, Lee's notions of poetry may strike the reader as what might conventionally be called mystical, but mystical in an everyday context. As he tells Marie Jordan, it is possible to experience the presence of an eternal mystery while folding the laundry.

Once again, Lee is a poet who takes his vocation very seriously. Being a poet, he says, is a 24-hour-a-day job. The poet must be continually prepared: "When a poem happens," as he says, at any time, day or night, he must be ready for its "allness" to manifest itself in words. He can say, without a bit of embarrassment, that "a poem is embodied passion." At the same time, the poem itself is the process of its own making, not the material form it might take on a sheet of paper. Indeed, he likes to repeat the anecdote of the Chinese poet Li-po, who often finished writing his poems and then folded them into the shapes of boats to sail down a nearby stream. Lee is also drawn to the model of Tibetan sand paintings whose artistic fragility reminds their creator that art is the creative process itself, not so much its end-products, the artifacts our culture warehouses in museums and libraries as art. In an aesthetic version of the popularized notion of chaos theory, Lee proposes that the very composition of the poem changes the external world, even if no one reads the poem. Drawing on what W. B. Yeats said in defense of his practice of ceaselessly revising his poems—"It is myself that I remake"—Lee focuses on the process itself of producing the poem, rather than the finished poem as product. Once again, to draw on his paradigm of Emily Dickinson, he asserts that in writing a poem he is attempting to achieve the being of Dickinson when she wrote her poems.

The conversations in this collection have a special value because Li-Young Lee has never been an academic and has little interest in the kind of discourse to which academic poets are often more attuned. Lee is just not likely to write essays, explaining his notions of his craft as a poet. As these conversations make clear, this is not to say that he has nothing to add to the contemporary discourse about writing poetry. In the Cooper and Yu interview Lee talks about an occasion on which he was persuaded to give a public lecture. His experience, as he himself seems very aware, probably would not have happened to, say, Gerald Stern but might well have driven Emily Dickinson from the stage. A lively and articulate speaker, Lee was literally left dumbstruck by the challenge of talking *at* an audience of hundreds. At the suggestion of his editor, Al Poulin, he started to read and talk about his poems, and when the audience left they were probably better satisfied by Lee's gesture of vulnerability and genuine personhood than if he had talked on for an hour about contempo-rary poetics. Essentially this collection offers what Lee does best—other than write poems, of course. The conversations allow him to read his poems and talk about the context in which he recalls writing them. When an interviewer commented on his practice–a practice shared with many other contemporary poets during public readings–of talking about the poem before and after reading it, Lee's response was very telling: "The place I'm at when those poems arrive I experience as great vulnerability so that to read feels too vulnerable. I need something around the poems to make myself comfortable." Like his comments in public readings, Lee's remarks in these conversations have the function of also helping to make his readers feel comfortable when they share some of the poet's sense of vulnerability as the poems occur. This is a poet, after all, who tells us, "I want something so intimate that it's less than whispered."

These conversations offer access to Lee's sense of himself as a working poet and his concept of what it means to be a poet. We begin with the concerns that interviewers usually start out focusing on: the actual practice of the poem coming into being. Although he says that a poem might occur at anytime, for all practical purposes the writing of poetry for Lee is a night-shift. It is obviously no coincidence that his most recent collection of poems is entitled *Book of My Nights*. He speaks of the especially conducive atmosphere of his large Chicago home at night when all the generations of the extended family are asleep. He has his own kind of 9–5 job: "I work from about nine at night to five in the morning." Once all the distractions of daytime consciousness and the external life reduce themselves to a minimum, he moves into a state resembling what he terms trance, a state that is for him the opening out of unified being to the Greater Consciousness he identifies as God. In such a state the creation of the poem can call up awe in the poet, too, as he suggests in talking about his early poem, "The Cleaving": "The poem was a little terrifying for me to write, I think, because finally in order to see everybody in myself and to see myself in everybody I had to do violence to myself." Such talk might suggest that the poems simply occur to Lee and all that they require is a kind of poetic stenography. Nothing could be farther from the truth, for he is an indefatigable reviser. Speaking of the title poem, "The City in Which I Love You," he claims to have worked on revisions for years: "During the three years most of it was cutting and revising. It was originally about forty pages." Revising becomes a variety of archaeology, of retrieving the poem beneath the poem. Paradoxically, Lee testifies to the creative anxiety of waiting, *praying*, for the poem to begin to occur, to use his term, followed by the seemingly endless process of revising drafts of the poem. In the case of his memoir, *The Winged Seed*, he notes that instead of revising he started over and produced what amounted to dozens of long manuscripts, only one of which was actually published as the book itself.

One source of anxiety as he sits waiting for the poem to occur is a recognition that, once a word or image or line has started to generate itself as the poem, it eliminates, as he says, the other 999 or 9,999 poems that might have been produced. Furthermore, as he tells Cooper and Yu, "When I'm done writing a poem the knowledge it took to write that poem doesn't help me with the next one. . . . I start from scratch." Thus, when asked a standard interview question such as, "What suggestions do you have for a new poetry writer?" Lee is likely to voice his own sense of needing help: "I feel like a new poetry writer," and any experience he may have gained in writing hundreds of poems offers little to compensate for the sense of starting all over again with each new poem. Similarly, he has reservations about how much a beginning poet can actually learn in poetry-writing work-shops; for him at least, it has been more useful to focus on those he terms the "great poets" such as Dickinson or Li-po for whom "every poem they wrote was a new experience." What readers are likely to discover in Lee's remarks is an extraordinary freshness and vulner-ability, an invitation to join him in the intimate engagement with his poems and his unique sense of the poet's vocation.

There is some irony in Li-Young Lee's tendency to see himself as what we generally think of as a Young Poet. Even though he is still several years from his fiftieth birthday, he has published three books of poems and the memoir *The Winged Seed*. His first collection of poems, *Rose* (1986), won New York University's Delmore Schwartz Memorial Poetry Award. His second book, *The City in Which I Love You* (1990) was a Lamont Poetry Selection of the Academy of American Poets. His most recent *Book of My Nights* (2001) received the William Carlos Williams Award from the Poetry Society of America and has been well received; for example, the reviewer for *AsianWeek*, Roy Kamada, wrote that it "is a new book from one of the most essential poets and is not to be missed." He has been honored with the Academy for American Poets 69th Fellowship for distinguished poetic achievement. His poems also appear in *The Norton Anthology of American Literature*.

To these accomplishments, which would seem to contradict Lee's self-image as a poet who has not yet established a significant reputation, we might also note that he has participated in over two dozen interviews. Clearly his readers are extremely interested in what he has to say about his poems and his sense of what it means to be a poet. These interviews have appeared in important journals such as the *Indiana Review* and the *Kenyon Review* and in collections such as Bill Moyers's *The Language of Life: A Festival of Poets* and Tod Marshall's *Range of the Possible: Conversations with Contemporary Poets*. Some of the interviews, however, were published in smaller journals such as *Riksha* and *Crab Orchard Review*, while others have never appeared in print at all. In editing these interviews a serious attempt has been made to preserve the sense of the original conversation by seeking a middle ground beyond the looseness and wordiness of spoken English, on the one hand, and a print text that reads like an essay, on the other.

This collection brings together a dozen interviews that provide readers of Lee's poetry a sample of his provocative, witty, and engaging comments on his writing and what it means to be a kind of mystic in the 21st century. For a poet still some years away from a biography perhaps, this proposed collection of his interviews offers an early and intimate portrait of a poet who is passionate about the vocation that chose him.

Earl G. Ingersoll
Brockport, New York
October 2005

Seeing the Power of Poetry

William Heyen and Stan Sanvel Rubin

The following conversation took place 9 October 1987 during Lee's visit to the State University of New York College at Brockport. He spoke with poets William Heyen and Stan Sanvel Rubin. Printed by permission of the Brockport Writers Forum and Videotape Library.

Lee began with a reading of his poem "Mnemonic."

Mnemonic

I was tired. So I lay down.
My lids grew heavy. So I slept.
Slender memory, stay with me.

I was cold once. So my father took off his blue sweater,
He wrapped me in it, and I never gave it back.
It is the sweater he wore to America,
this one, which I've grown into, whose sleeves are too long,
whose elbows have thinned, who outlives its rightful owner.
Flamboyant blue in daylight, poor blue by daylight,
it is black in the folds.

A serious man who devised complex systems of numbers and
    rhymes
to aid him in remembering, a man who forgot nothing, my
    father
would be ashamed of me.
Not because I'm forgetful,

but because there is no order
to my memory, a heap
of details, uncatalogued, illogical.
For instance:
God was lonely. So he made me.
My father loved me. So he spanked me.
It hurt him to do so. He did it daily.

The earth is flat. Those who fall off don't return.
The earth is round. All things reveal themselves to men only
    gradually.

I won't last. Memory is sweet.
Even when it's painful, memory is sweet.

Once, I was cold. So my father took off his blue sweater.

Heyen: I like "Mnemonic" very much. It's a beautiful poem. There's a rhythm to memory, and you've captured it here. You say, or the voice of the poem says, "slender memory, stay with me," and then you go back to an incident with your father, you range around it, you remember despair—there's a lot of pain in the poem. Then you come back to this incident again. Awfully strong.

   To talk about a bigger thing within the poem: "My father loved me, so he spanked me. / It hurt him to do so. He did it daily." Even though the poem dwells on this pain and this hurt, you do swing upward; you do insist on saying, "Once I was cold. So my father took off his blue sweater." You've made a great circle back toward that again. It's a poem of praise and affirmation. Do you connect this with something you see poetry as wanting to do?

Lee: In the poem I wanted to do my father a kind of justice, and in a way myself a kind of justice. I wanted to come to terms with the same man who, of course, spanked me daily and who was capable of great tenderness. I also wanted to do myself a kind of justice, to establish that my memory isn't so much poor as it is that I'm baffled by events and I'm baffled by the need to catalog those events and make sense of them so that my life doesn't seem to be a series of disconnected episodes; it does reveal a kind of unfolding quality.

Heyen: The poem *aids* memory?

Lee: Yes, it helps me to remember, and it helps me give a continuity to my memories. Because I'm often *baffled* by them. I have memories that nobody else seems to share with me. And of course I have memories that are flawed. I remember certain situations, not wholly, and as a result I have to deal with this partial knowledge of my own past, or my family's past, and I have to come to terms with that. And the poem *helps* me do that. In this poem I'm trying to listen for that voice that is slowed down and finds the continuum that links these memories. That voice is absolutely important to me. It simultaneously *slows down* the onrush of memories and makes some sense of them—not necessarily great *meaning* or profundity out of them, just some sense, in a life which would otherwise be *baffling* to me.

Heyen: Stafford says sometimes his idea of the poem is that he says something to see what the effect will be of his having said it. I have that kind of feeling sometimes, too: you'll say something to see how you'll react to what it is you've said about your father, for example: "My father would be ashamed of me." And then the mind of the poem dwells on that possibility—not as a locked-in thing, but as a possibility to get to the next thing that's going to be said.

Lee: I *love* what Stafford says. I've thought about that a lot. For me that's also important to the feeling that the poem isn't a meeting of a form, an agenda, but it is an unfolding, a discovery, as I write it. And, of course, hopefully as I later read it, it continues to unfold for me. So the poem in *time* is very important. It's not something I've set down on a page, and it's an object now, but it's continuing to unfold in time. Its existence in the time-frame is very important.

Heyen: I think if the poem doesn't continue to talk to you, either you're a poor reader or the poem is too frozen in its positions.

Tell us about your beginnings as a writer, your place as a son in a family where poetry did matter, where a father loved poetry.

Lee: My mother and father had a classical Chinese education, which meant they each had to memorize by graduation 300 poems from the T'ang Dynasty. I grew up hearing my parents recite Chinese poems. And seeing that poetry could bring tears to a person's eyes, or my mother would be cutting vegetables and suddenly stop, while we were talking, and say, Now listen to this, and she would speak a very moving poem—that to me was very important. I could see that poetry wasn't something that we talked loftily about, but something you spoke while cutting vegetables with your child. And of course my father being a minister I had the King James Bible read to me and I read it myself; and I *heard* it read from the pulpit. When I witnessed that, I felt it was a great feeling of power. For me poetry is both those things: that power and yet some mundane—in the best sense—some mundane thing we do.

Rubin: Would you say something a bit more biographical, or autobiographical, about your early experiences. You were born of Chinese descent in Indonesia in a particularly bad time.

Lee: While we were in Indonesia, my father fell out of favor with the Sukarno regime and was imprisoned for nineteen months on a leper colony. I remember visiting him there, by boat. I remember strange things like that that I could never make sense out of—until recently, having the courage to ask my mother about these things. And of course we traveled a lot. We escaped from Indonesia. You know, now that I'm talking about this, I suddenly remember something: my father at one point read to me a letter that a group of his associates had written to him, a farewell letter. They were planning their own escape, and they wrote this farewell letter they all signed at the bottom; they quoted a poem—I believe it was one of the ancient Chinese—and I remember the last two lines. It says something like: "With China our home and Heaven our neighborhood, why would you stand at the fork in the road, crying like a heart-broken child?" These friends of his got on the boat, they tried to escape, and they were all subsequently caught and put to death. But he read that letter to me, and he read those lines to me in Chinese. He was so moved. Again I saw the power of poetry. So I think poetry came early in my life, and the power of the written word. I remember the letter was written very beautifully. That was right before *we* had escaped from Indonesia. We traveled a little bit in Japan and Macao—we were fleeing, actually, not traveling—and we later came to America. We moved around in America a little bit, and my father attended seminary, before we settled in a small town in Western Pennsylvania.

Rubin: How many of you were there?

Lee: Let's see. I have a brother my parents left in China during the violence that had gone on there. They had to leave him: he was very ill, he couldn't be moved. They were planning to go back when things cleared up. They didn't know it was going to take 26 years for things to clear up. So I have a brother that we just got out about ten years ago. While we were doing the traveling there was my sister, my two other brothers, and my mother and father.

Rubin: When you came to this country how did you first experience the English-American literary tradition? What was that like?

Lee: I remember Seattle, Washington, the first place we came to. I remember hearing a lot of ethnic slurs. I didn't understand them, of course, but later on as I picked up more and more English I knew they were ethnic slurs.

The first phrase I learned in English was "Shut up," and that's the only thing I knew.

I had a problem speaking—maybe this contributes to poetry, I always like to think it does, at least to my poetry—I didn't say anything the first three years of my life. Then on the night of our escape, about three miles out of harbor, I spoke in complete sentences. I spoke for about fifteen minutes, nonstop, and then I stopped entirely. Since then I haven't spoken Indonesian.

I think that says something about poetry. I like to think I was internalizing all that language.

Heyen: And what do you remember about your own first poems? When did you begin writing?

Lee: In college. I had taken a workshop with Ed Ochester. I needed three credits. I remember him saying, "I just want you to write a lot." I wasn't used to being given that kind of license; I was studying biochemistry at the time. So of course everybody was producing a lot, and I had a hard time coming to terms with that. I had thought there was supposed to be some kind of *agenda*—I was supposed to write sonnets, or something—but soon I began to tap into what was important to me, my own life, and that's when I began writing.

Heyen: That's my sense of this book *Rose*. It's your first book, but it's as though it's your second book. Very often in first books American poets write poems about those things that they think poems are written about. Very often it's with their second—or even later—books that they begin to tap into things genuinely important to them. You've gone past the apprentice stage all at once. A few minutes ago you were saying, "Now that I'm talking about this, I suddenly remember something," and you began to tell a story. That's my sense of this book: it begins talking to itself, and it delves and spirals down and interconnects and keeps spiraling around some central memories.

I made just a brief list for myself here of the central things—beyond motif they reach symbol—that this book is about: water, rose, rain, hair, father. And all of these things have "r" sounds and mnemonically keep circling on themselves.

Lee: Thank you, Bill. I'm glad you feel that way. I do have the sense that poetry is more than a polite activity, that it *feeds* me. When I came to America I discovered that the people who are the most tolerant with ethnic groups are cultured people. When I say, "cultured" I don't mean people who know which fork to use on which side of the plate. I mean really *cultured* people, people who have a global view of the world, and they get that global view from art. And I don't say "art" meaning what's polite and hung up in galleries and appreciated. I mean the artistic life, the creative life. For me "culture" isn't becoming a refined citizen so much as becoming a refined soul, a refined spirit. Poetry to me is never a hobby. It's not something we do with one eye closed or we do in our spare time; it's something you give your life to, something you live by. And it has to come out of what you live by. That's why the poems in this book [*Rose*] arise out of my love for people, for my bafflement before people and before the world.

Rubin: How, in fact, did the poems in *Rose* come to be this book?

Lee: Actually there are a lot of poems that I threw out. Now that I look at it and it's so thin I wish I would have put more in. But I just couldn't. I'm such a slow writer. I think for somebody who writes this way the danger is writing anecdotes, and I suppose I had a lot of those that I just threw out. Emerson says something about man being an alembic and nature passes through him and becomes art. And I love that. A lot of those I threw out weren't poems because nature hadn't passed through me to become art. It was just raw nature, the recording of interesting anecdotes.

Rubin: What thought did you give to the book's two parts?

Lee: I suppose there was a naiveté the poems in the first section speak to or speak from. I'm hoping that the poems in the last section and the long poem, "Always a Rose," speak to a kind of education of the spirit. Of course, I don't mean formal education. I mean a coming to terms, fierce terms even, with certain aspects of my life, and my father's life. That's what I was hoping it would do by being broken up this way. I don't know if that kind of ferocity comes out.

Rubin: Could you say something about the title *Rose*? Although there is no one poem entitled "Rose" in the book, the rose image seems to run throughout.

Lee: When I was very young my father used to tell me, Life is like a great big flower, and it keeps opening and opening and opening perpetually. He was a great rose-gardener, and he loved roses. And of course there is, in fact, a Chinese dish where you cook roses. Also the Chinese cook roses for medicinal purposes. My mother was a great rose-cooker; she used to fry them and make them taste like grapes. And it was odd for me to find out in *Natural History* Pliny talks about the medicinal purposes of roses, too. I become quite obsessed with roses ever since my father gave me that image of the flower opening and opening.

Rubin: The cover of the book [*Rose*] is, in fact, a rendering of a sort of flower, presumably a rose.

Lee: My brother did a painting, and we got the cover from that. Actually he began by doing a Chinese calligraphy brush-stroke of the word *flower*, and it kept evolving into something else.

Rubin: I would ask you to read the poem "Dreaming of Hair," and since we're on the topic of images that matter to you you might say something about "hair" in your work.

Lee: OK, there are two allusions here. As I have said, when I was quite small I was reading the King James Bible, and two stories in particular really stuck with me: the story of Samson and the story of Absalom. Of course we know the story of Samson. The particular allusion here is where Delilah seduces him, weaves his hair into a loom, thinking that it would weaken him, but of course his hair bursts out of the loom and he's strong again. And the story of Absalom, who's an extremely beautiful young man, with long, flowing locks, as the Bible describes him. He tries to usurp his father David's kingdom, and when he fails he runs away. As he's riding through an orchard his beautiful, long hair gets caught in the boughs. David's warlords surround him, and they look at him and jeer at him. Then they slay him. For me the image of hair was one of great power in the case of Samson—but a kind of dumb power, too, because in fact Samson isn't very interesting as a character, except that he's very strong—and the notion of Absalom whose hair was an image of beauty and doom. So I walked around with that all my life, and of course all the women in my life have very long, black hair.

Hair

Ivy ties the cellar door
in autumn, in summer morning glory
wraps the ribs of a mouse.
Love binds me to the one
whose hair I've found in my mouth,
whose sleeping head I kiss,
wondering is it death?
beauty? this dark
star spreading in every direction from the crown of her head.

My love's hair is autumn hair, there
the sun ripens.
My fingers harvest the dark
vegetable of her body.
In the morning I remove it
from my tongue and
sleep again.

Hair spills
through my dream, sprouts from my stomach, thickens my heart,
and tangles the brain. Hair ties the tongue dumb.
Hair ascends the tree
of my childhood—the willow

I climbed
one bare foot and hand at a time,
feeling the knuckles of the gnarled tree, hearing
my father plead from his window, *Don't fall!*

In my dream I fly
past summers and moths
to the thistle
caught in my mother's hair, the purple one
I touched and bled for,
to myself at three, sleeping
beside her, waking with her hair in my mouth.

Along a slippery twine of her black hair
my mother ties *ko-tze* knots for me;
fish and lion heads, chrysanthemum buds, the heads
of Chinamen, black-haired and frowning.

Li-En, my brother, frowns when he sleeps.
I push back hair, stroke his brow.
His hairline is our father's, three peaks pointing down.

What sprouts from the body
and touches the body?
What filters sunlight
and drinks moonlight?
Where have I misplaced my heart?
What stops wheels and great machines?
What tangles in the bough
and snaps the loom?

Out of the grave
my father's hair
bursts. A strand
pierces my left sole, shoots
up bone, past ribs,
to the broken heart it stitches,
then down,

swirling in the stomach, in the groin, and down,
through the right foot.

What binds me to this earth?
What remembers the dead
and grows toward them?

I'm tired of thinking.
I long to taste the world with a kiss.
I long to fly into hair with kisses and weeping,
remembering an afternoon
when, kissing my sleeping father, I saw for the first time
behind the thick swirl of his black hair,
the mole of wisdom,
a lone planet spinning slowly.

Sometimes my love is melancholy
and I hold her head in my hands.
Sometimes I recall our hair grows after death.
Then, I must grab handfuls
of her hair, and, I tell you, there
are apples, walnuts, ships sailing, ships docking, and men
taking off their boots, their hearts breaking,
not knowing
which they love more, the water, or
their women's hair, sprouting from the head, rushing toward
    the feet.

When I made those allusions I didn't mean to say that I wrote
this poem out of a literary context. But the Bible for me was very real;
I wasn't reading literature. And I certainly wasn't reading only a
religious tract. To me those stories were very real. When I watched my
father braid my mother's hair, and he did it every night, I could see
how he was in love with her hair, and these stories would come back
to me. There were all kinds of reverberations. I guess the point I'm
trying to make is that literature or poetry for me isn't a "literary
event"; it's not relegated to some world in books or schoolrooms. It's
living.

Heyen: You compose a world for yourself there. You keep staring at and meditating on and entering into something that is involved with your deepest being. This is essentially inviting your soul to observe at ease a spear of summer grass, and that seems to be an act of this book. You do that very often in these not-quite "catalog poems," these definition poems that keep giving of themselves as you keep looking into them.

Lee: As a matter of fact, Walt Whitman is *extremely* important to me. I discovered him late. When I first found Walt Whitman, I didn't like him. He's not an easy poet. People think he's an easy poet, and they kind of banish him that way. As a young person I didn't understand him. His kind of expansive spiritual appetite, or spiritual productivity, is a very mature thing. In "Song of the Broad Ax," the way he moves from the description of the ax and the wooden handle to the shapes of democracy *astounded* me with the movements a poem could make, and then he began to make a lot of sense to me. My doorway to Whitman perhaps *was* the King James Bible, where they *are* stories that enlarge, and grow small and minute and detailed, and then grow large again. Whitman didn't make sense to me until quite late; as a matter of fact he began to make sense to me during the writing of the longer poems, where I do that kind of meditating.

Heyen: I call you, too, a "poet of inclusion." It's as though you want everything in your poems.

Lee: I do want everything. In that moment of knowing when you're writing, certainly not a conscious knowing, I want to know everything. I want everything to get in there: I have this huge appetite.

Heyen: And that wanting to know everything gets to be a terrible burden, too, doesn't it? You say, "I'm tired of thinking. I long to taste the world with a kiss." To what extent do you insist on understanding what it is that goes on in your poem? What does this word *understanding* mean when it comes to poetry?

Lee: I know that I understand it . . . intuitively, and that's all I care to. That's about all I ask of myself. I don't want to get my little red pen out and start taking it apart. I took a friend to an art exhibit; it was an installation art piece. I believe it was Joseph Beuys. We took the subway to a very seedy part of Chicago. We got off the subway—it was about five o'clock, the streets were empty, it was snowing—and we knocked on a big freight door. A man in a security uniform slides the door open and says, "What do you want?" and I said, "We're here to see the Joseph Beuys exhibit." He said, "Come with me," and we walk into this huge, empty warehouse. We walk and walk and walk to the other side where he opens this tiny, little wooden door, and we walk through this narrow, little hallway, and he opens another door and there's another huge warehouse. Then he goes to the other side, and we're walking all the time, and my friend is baffled. He goes to another tiny, little door that we have to stoop to go through, and he says, "Here it is." And there's a brick wall, gold-leafed, and there's a hat rack with a coat and hat there. The guard says, "Well, that's it. Take a look." So we took a look. He says, "Had enough?" and we said, "Yeah." So we turn around and walk out. My friend and I were talking about it, and he says, "I didn't understand it." And I made the comment he *would* understand it if I told him we're no longer awake; what we're going to experience now is a dream. There's a logic to dreaming. We don't ask the same logic of dreams that we ask of life. So I don't think we should ask the same kind of logic and understanding of poems that we do of life. I think I'm moving in a different element when I'm reading or writing poems. I don't ask the same things of them.

Rubin: What do you ask of your readers, though? How do you think of your readers, if you do, in the process of writing?

Lee: I have two answers to that. The first one I'm a little bit ashamed of: I *have*, in fact, a handful of readers that I think about. When I'm writing the poem, I keep thinking, Oh, if so-and-so sees this, then they'll really think I'm a poet. I always have this feeling I want to prove I'm a poet myself to a handful of people. On the other hand, all I ask is that readers are "soul-awake." I got that term from you, Bill. The reader has to be prepared for what gets them. That's all; it's not much. It's not much, but it's an awful lot.

Rubin: To go back to the notion that there's some connection perhaps between the poem and dream, when you're writing are you caught up in a kind of reverie, do you find the words just come at some point? Do you, in fact, revise very much?

Lee: Oh, I revise *heavily*. Probably too much.

Rubin: How would you describe the process of writing?

Lee: You know, something makes me want to say, "It's language-generated." But at the same time, that kind of talk frightens me. Because if it's "language-generated," then what happens to the world? Suddenly that just wipes the world out. And I have to say that I'm concerned just as much with ideas and with making sense of my world as I am with language. It isn't mere *play* for me. I can't say, "A line comes to me." I've heard friends say that a line will come to them and they're writing just to understand that line. I can understand where they're coming from, but at the same time it can't have any philosophical importance to me that way. I mean, what are we doing? We're just playing around here? We're playing with verbs and nouns? For me it can't exist that way. I suppose when the world gets into my blood it finds a way of expressing itself. When nature has passed through me as an alembic it comes out as art.

Rubin: You told me earlier you speak your poems aloud as you write them?

Lee: I read them aloud as I'm writing them.

Heyen: Writing the poem is always at least two things at once, isn't it? That is, trying to see what it is that you're doing and at the same time not to be diminished by certain kinds of rationality and logic. I've sensed this again and again in *Rose*, as in the "Mnemonic" poem when you say, "And this is true, the Earth is flat," and then you say, "And this is true, the Earth is round." There's constantly an insistence on that. Or, in the "Dreaming Hair" poem, the vision of the hair from your dead father piercing your left foot and knitting your heart. There are constantly things going on in this book that say, I am not going to be a slave to the world of one plus one equals two because there's something more to it than that. Emerson said, "The one thing of value, in this world, is the active soul." That's the sense I get of this, knowing always, too, that there's another world beyond this one to which and of which the poem is trying to talk.

Lee: The Chinese have a saying: We should try to live our life so that it's big enough to contain all the paradoxes. I suppose the attempt I make in a poem, too, is to contain its own paradox.

Heyen: I'd hate to be mnemonic here, but it seems to me that's the only vision that can save us—"the vision of the great One is myriad," Ginsberg says in "Wales Visitation." It's when we're being "democratic," in Walt's sense, and loving the worm and loving the woman and loving the tree, that poetry tells us we'll stop killing the earth and killing one another.

Lee: I'd like to say something about that, though. When people hear that, they think that's some kind of liberal gushiness. For me that's a *real* hard spiritual task. That's a hard thing to do, to become *that* democratic, *that* eclectic. It's not just a matter of dabbling in the world; it's a matter of really embracing it spiritually, and I think that's a hard, hard thing to do. And I think it's a hard thing to do in poems, and that's what makes Whitman so great.

Heyen: It's difficult to love.

Lee: To love is very difficult.

A Well of Dark Waters

Bill Moyers

From The Language of Life: A Festival of Poets *by Bill Moyers, copyright © 1995 by Public Affairs Television, Inc. And David Grubin Productions, Inc. Used by permission of Doubleday, a division of Random House, Inc. Lee appeared in the Moyers PBS series* The Power of the Word *in 1988.*

Moyers: How do you answer when people ask, "Where are you from?"

Lee: I say Chicago, then I tell them I was born in Indonesia, but I'm adamant about insisting that, although I was born in Indonesia, I'm Chinese. I don't want them to think that I'm Indonesian—my people were persecuted by the Indonesians.

Moyers: Your great-grandfather was the first president of the People's Republic of China.

Lee: Yes. He's my mother's grandfather and, of course, my mother's family—the House of Yuan—fell into demise during Mao's cultural revolution. Because my mother came from royalty and my father's father was a gangster and an entrepreneur, my parents' marriage was very frowned upon in China. When they got married they started traveling, and they finally fled to Indonesia, where my father had taught medicine and philosophy at Gamaliel University in Jakarta. Later on he was incarcerated by Sukarno because of his Western leanings. My father loved Western theology and Western literature. He was teaching the King James Bible there as literature, and when interest in Western culture fell out of favor he was locked up.

I was born in 1957, and he was locked up in 1958 and kept in prison for nineteen months. When he escaped we fled Indonesia and traveled throughout Indochina and Southeast Asia for several years before winding up in Hong Kong, where he became an evangelist minister and head of a hugely successful, million dollar business. But he was driven almost solely by emotion and at one point got into an argument with somebody and simply left Hong Kong. We just left it all and came to America.

Moyers: And what did he do then?

Lee: He took whatever money he had in his bank account, a couple thousand dollars, and my mother sold the jewelry off her body to get us through the first few years. We went from Seattle, where he was a greeter at the China exhibit at the Seattle World's Fair, to Pittsburgh, where he studied theology at the seminary there. He got his degree and became a Presbyterian minister at a very small church in Vandergrift, Pennsylvania.

Moyers: What a story! From that rich, complex Oriental culture to a small American town.

Lee: Yes. I always thought there was something tragic about it, but he loved it. He loved the church and he loved the town we lived in. He loved being a pastor.

Moyers: Why did the story of his life strike you as tragic?

Lee: He was a man of huge intellectual and artistic talents. He was reading and translating the Bible and Kierkegaard, and he loved Shakespeare and opera. Then he came to a basically working-class town where, although there were many beautiful and wonderful people, I think his intellectual life almost stopped, or it wasn't fed. But he seemed not to mind—he told me when he was very ill that he was tired of running around so much and that's why he loved being there.

Moyers: Your journey—China, Indonesia, Hong Kong, Macao, Japan, Seattle, Pittsburgh—is a story of the twentieth century, the century of refugees.

Lee: In a way, I feel as if our experience may be no more than an outward manifestation of a homelessness that people in general feel. It seems to me that anybody who thinks about our position in the universe cannot help but feel a little disconnected and homeless, so I don't think we're special. We refugees might simply express outwardly what all people feel inwardly.

Moyers: Do you feel yourself an exile?

Lee: In my most pessimistic moods I feel that I'm disconnected and that I'm going to be disconnected forever, that I'll never have any place that I can call home. For example, I find it strange that when I go to visit my father's grave I look down and there on his stone is the Chinese character for his name and, when I look up, there are all these American flags on the other graves. So I feel a little strange, but I don't know what it is. I don't feel nostalgic because I don't know what to feel nostalgic *for*. It's simply a feeling of disconnection and dislocation.

Moyers: What is there about exodus and exile that gives some poets a special power?

Lee: I don't know. Exile seems both a blessing and a curse. A lot of my friends who are writers have said to me, "You're so lucky to have this background to write from," and I guess in a way I *am* lucky, but I wouldn't wish that experience on anybody. The literature I love most is the literature of ruins and the experience of exodus. I don't know why but, for example, the Book of Exodus is very important to me— the wandering of the children of Israel has profound resonance for me. I don't feel as if those stories are about a primitive tribe in some distant desert. That struggle for belief and faith in the face of humiliation, annihilation, apostasy—all that seems to me really what I go through and what we *all* go through, finally.

Moyers: How did you become a poet?

Lee: In my household my father read to us constantly from the King James Bible, and because he had a classical Chinese education, which meant he had memorized three hundred poems from the T'ang Dynasty, he would recite those poems to us as well and we would recite them back to him. My memory was so bad I could never do very well, but I *did* learn to love poetry.

When I heard him read from the pulpit from Psalms and Proverbs, I would think, My God, that's incredible! What power! then

I would hear people in the congregation. I don't know if other faiths do this, but Presbyterians have a responsive reading where the minister reads a passage and the congregation responds by reading another passage—steelworkers, schoolteachers, all of us together saying, "Make a joyful noise unto the Lord, all ye lands." That seemed magical to me and entirely beautiful, but I never thought I could write it.

I thought poetry was some high and mighty thing of the angels and of the ancient dead in China. Later on, when I met Gerald Stern at the University of Pittsburgh, I read his poetry, and I suddenly realized that poetry could be written by living human beings. Then he became my teacher and I tried doing it myself.

Moyers: Both of you write about exodus and ruins.

Lee: Yes. When I first opened his book *Lucky Life*, I expected small anecdotal poems—that's what we were taught to expect in modern poetry—but I suddenly thought I was reading something out of the Psalms or Lamentations. I walked around with *Lucky Life* in my pocket for two years—that book was just in tatters.

Moyers: Well, the fact is that you were the son of a New Testament preacher and you were tutored by an Old Testament prophet— Gerald Stern is a prophet in shirt sleeves—so it's no surprise that I hear so much of the Bible in your poems.

Lee: Oh, I *love* the Bible. I adore it. I love it as literature—the stories, the drama, the largeness, the characters—and I love the wisdom in it.

Moyers: So many of your early poems in particular deal with your father.

Lee: He was for me a huge character. He made it obvious early on that he was the template by which all his sons and his daughter were to measure our lives. He always set himself up as a goal for us, and he wasn't modest about it. He impressed upon us that we were supposed to speak seven languages, as he did; but I only speak two—Mandarin Chinese and English. He told us that we should be able to translate Kierkegaard and the Psalms. A few years ago I actually thought that I was going to study Hebrew and translate the Psalms before I realized that was merely another quarrel I was still having with my dead father.

Moyers: Are you able to let go of your father as a subject? Do you think you've written your last poem about him? Have you settled that old quarrel?

Lee: I don't think I've settled that old quarrel, but I think for the good of my own writing, I have had to force myself to look beyond him, although in a way I'm being guided again by him to look at things that were important to him. I'd like to write about my own struggle with belief and disbelief, and I'd like to write my own experiences as an immigrant and refugee.

Moyers: Did you ever feel devastated by him, as some sons do by a strong father?

Lee: No! You know, that's the one thing I have no doubt about. My mother once pointed to me and said, "You are the stone on which your father's patience broke." I realized that she was talking about a great deal of strength that I got from both my mother and father and that a part of him broke against me. Of course, she didn't tell me that until he was dead, but I realized that I had a lot of strength to be able to stand up against him. I never wanted to leave home. I always knew that I would only grow stronger by struggling against him, and I was never afraid of him. I was in awe, but I never feared him.

Moyers: There's so much tenderness that comes through in your poems about him.

Lee: He was an infinitely tender man. I remember a day—I think we were living in Hong Kong at the time—when he came rushing home, very excited, with a small, brown paper bag. He had discovered Worcestershire sauce. He had the servants move all of our living-room furniture out onto the lawn and cook a meal, then he doused everything with this sauce, and we ate out on the lawn. He was an exuberant kind of wild man, and he was infinitely tender.

The Gift

To pull the metal splinter from my palm
my father recited a story in a low voice.
I watched his lovely face and not the blade.

Before the story ended, he'd removed
The iron sliver I thought I'd die from.

I can't remember the tale
but hear his voice still, a well
of dark water, a prayer.
And I recall his hands,
two measures of tenderness
he laid against my face,
the flames of discipline
he raised above my head.

Had you entered that afternoon
you would have thought you saw a man
planting something in a boy's palm,
a silver tear, a tiny flame.
Had you followed that boy
you would have arrived here,
where I bend over my wife's right hand.

Look how I shave her thumbnail down
so carefully she feels no pain.
Watch as I lift the splinter out.
I was seven when my father
took my hand like this,
and I did not hold that shard
between my fingers and think,
Metal that will bury me,
christen it Little Assassin,
Ore Going Deep for My heart.
And I did not lift up my wound and cry,
Death visited here!
I did what a child does
When he's given something to keep.
I kissed my father.

Moyers: I'm touched by "The Gift." Tell me why you wrote it.

Lee: I was with my wife in a hotel and I woke up and heard her sobbing. I looked for her and she was sitting on the edge of the bathtub, sobbing and holding her hand. I noticed that her hand was bleeding, and when I looked there was a splinter under her thumbnail. My father was dead at the time, but when I bent down to remove the splinter I realized that I had learned that tenderness from my father.

Moyers: And the gift was?

Lee: I suppose it was a lesson, a gift of tenderness that he gave to me and that I was able to give to somebody else.

Moyers: You've written that you really discovered most about your father when you opened his Bible after his death and read his notations in the margin.

Lee: I inherited all his books, and when I opened his Bible one day and began reading it, and also reading the marginalia—all the things he had written in the margins of the book—it was like experiencing his mind at work, and I realized it was a fierce, questioning mind. When he was teaching us he always seemed so sure—he never questioned anything; everything that came out of his mouth was spit out in hard, pithy statements—and then when I opened his Bible and saw there were questions and underlinings and references to other books I realized he was struggling to come to terms with his own belief, and I really grasped another dimension of him.

I also realized that basically I didn't know him, and that both of us were at fault. He put up a huge front, the front of a man who would not be questioned. He would *always* be right, he would *always* be sure. And I suppose that comes from his experience of imprisonment and wandering—he wanted his children to have faith in him. He didn't want us to be afraid, so he had to keep up that front.

But by the same token, it didn't make me ever feel I had a human being for a father. He was always right next to God. There was an hour each day when we had to be very quiet because he was praying in his study, and I remember thinking, Jeez, he's in there convening with this being who is like no being that I know. So for an hour we had to observe this silence and tiptoe around him. That's the way it was in our house.

Moyers: But when you opened the Bible the man you found there was less austere, less dogmatic, less cocksure?

Lee: Exactly. For example, he always talked to us about the Song of Songs as if it were a song between the Church and God. Then when I read his Bible I realized he read it very explicitly as a poem about sexuality. He would refer to other poems about sexuality and he had underlined his favorite passages and written out little love poems in the corners of the pages. Finding all that was an incredible experience. I realized he was a man who was saying one thing but who was living another life.

Early in the Morning

While the long grain is softening
in the water, gurgling
over a low stove flame, before
the salted Winter Vegetable is sliced
for breakfast, before the birds,
my mother glides an ivory comb
through her hair, heavy
and black as calligrapher's ink.

She sits at the foot of the bed.
My father watches, listens for
the music of comb
against hair.

My mother combs,
pulls her hair back
tight, rolls it
around two fingers, pins it
in a bun to the back of her head.
For half a hundred years she has done this.
My father likes to see it like this.
He says it is kempt.

But I know
it is because of the way
my mother's hair falls
when he pulls the pins out.

Easily, like the curtains
when they untie them in the evening.

Moyers: What about your mother?

Lee: As I said earlier, my mother was the great-granddaughter of Yuan Shi-Kai, and she was classically educated, but she doesn't speak much English. She lives with us. It was a lifelong dream for all of us to live together, so my brother and sister and my mother and my family all live in one house. I think she's an incredibly resilient woman, though she's become very reclusive since my father has died. She's a beautiful woman, and there was a point when she had hair down to the back of her knees.

Moyers: Does she ever talk about what it was like to have been a member of the Royal Family of China?

Lee: Occasionally she experiences a kind of nostalgia, but I think she has the feeling that we're in America now and that history is not going to help us. I grew up with the feeling that those stories about the House of Yuan and all the grandeur were simply stories. My father found it important to tell us stories about both families, but my mother was basically very reticent about her story. I don't know whether she was too sad about it or whether it didn't interest her, but even now when I ask her about what it was like growing up like that, she doesn't like to talk about it.

Moyers: Will you ever return to China?

Lee: I wonder about China, but I have no immediate plans to return there. My mother returned and found the family graves dug up, and she was told the bones were scattered—that happened during the Cultural Revolution—so in a way I feel there's nothing to return to. From what I understand, everything has been confiscated. They lived in a huge mansion, which has been turned into a small hospital, and certain parts of the land they owned have been turned into public parks, so I don't have any ruins to go back to, and it seems to me important that I should have ruins. I mean, shouldn't we? I have friends who have French, Spanish, or Italian backgrounds, and they go to Europe and I suppose they can connect. But if I go to Europe I would feel as if I'm going to look at somebody else's ruins, and if I go to China I'd also be looking at somebody else's ruins. I have the feeling I need to get back to Indonesia and yet, I don't know what I would look for there either. I'm not sure what I am supposed to look for anywhere.

I'm afraid to say that often my longing for home becomes a longing for heaven—instead of casting myself backwards, I take the impulse and cast it ahead—and yet, I question my own belief constantly. You know, I don't know if I believe in a heaven or a hell. But there's a longing in me for heaven. Maybe my longing for home comes from a longing for heaven.

Moyers: What are your favorite books in the Bible?

Lee: I think the Book of Exodus is my favorite, but the books of poetry I most like would be The Song of Songs and Ecclesiastes. On gloomy days I tell myself, I just want to write something like Ecclesiastes. And on happy days I think, I'm going to write The Song of Songs. Whoever put those two books side by side was definitely wise. We go from one extreme to another—a celebration of sexual love and then a kind of diatribe about the futility of life in general—but those are my two favorite books. If I could pinpoint what I want to do in my writing, I'd like to write something someday that would own the kind of scope and grandeur and intensity of those two books.

Moyers: When you read the Bible, what do you find out about yourself?

Lee: I identify with *all* the characters. For a while I was reading the Abraham and Isaac story, and I read that as my father as Abraham and me as Isaac. Then later on I read the story of Jacob and the Angel as a good metaphor for poetry, that somehow it's the struggle between the longing for heaven and the longing to stay on earth. I discover that there's a great longing in me to believe. I wouldn't say I believe, but I *want* to believe. I want badly to believe in a God, in a palpable God. I don't sense a palpable God, but as I'm reading the Bible, *that's* what I want.

Moyers: There are a lot of "outsiders" in the Bible. Exiles, seekers, rejected and despised.

Lee: Exactly. For a while I began to really rebel against Christianity, but when I realized that it began as a slave religion and that Christ was an outsider, then it began to make more sense to me.

Moyers: It seems to me that you are struggling in the same way your father was.

Lee: If I didn't know that he had struggled, I would always be questioning myself, asking, Why aren't I as strong as he was?

Moyers: But what you found in the margins of his Bible were the tracks of his own doubt.

Lee: Which helps me. Doubt is OK. In a way, I guess I'm affirming God by my doubt.

Moyers: Let's talk about the craft of writing poetry. How do you put a poem together?

Lee: For me, all the work *precedes* the actual writing of the poem and requires a kind of supplication, assuming a vulnerable posture, keeping open. It's like prayer. I think one has to do a lot of struggling before one actually kneels and says the words. Then after that, of course, there's a lot of revision; but I do a lot of reading and mental, spiritual, and emotional struggling before I actually come to the page.

When I *do* get to the page, it usually begins with a line that I can't make any sense of. Then I write to find out what that line means. I hate to sound as if language doesn't refer to something. In fact, I come to the page with certain experiences and intentions, but the poem begins to happen in a line, and I write to understand that.

Moyers: I hear you are now writing about your own children. Are they growing up thoroughly American?

Lee: I can see that they're in a way headed for doom because they're crazily dislocated. They're growing up in a household where both Chinese and English are spoken. At this point, they only speak English but they understand Chinese. If they walk into a room and there's a Chinese opera on the television, they'll sit down and watch these crazy antics, so they're already growing up dislocated. The older one said, "I'm Chinese, right?" I said, "Yes, you're *half* Chinese." He said, "And I'm half regular?" So there's Chinese and regular— he's already crazy with this stuff.

Moyers: Do you tell them stories?

Lee: Yes, I tell them stories constantly, and they love to hear stories. I used to tell them the basic stories, and then I ran out of those so I started making up stories in which the bad guy's name is Sukarno and the good guy's name is Yeh, which means grandfather in Chinese. Now they say, "Tell us the Sukarno stories."

Moyers: Do you tell them the story of your own family's fugitive travels?

Lee: Those are in fact the stories that I tell them. I make them sound more fairytale-like for them, but those stories are the only ones I know.

Moyers: Stories are crucial to the memories of exiles. They tell these stories over and over again. The stories often become scripture.

Lee: Yes. And that's the beauty of the Bible too—it's insistence on the importance of memory. The injunction *Zakhor* occurs more than one hundred times in the Bible, so that is important to me. Part of the problem refugees encounter is that as those stories are told again and again, from generation to generation, sometimes they're changed, so each time we're getting farther and farther away from factual reality, but I think the stories still adhere to an emotional and spiritual reality.

Moyers: What's the spiritual reality of your own family's journey.

Lee: Ah, God. I don't know. I'm sad to say this, but I think we all feel dislocated and that's why we want to live together. I think the spiritual reality of my family is dislocation, disconnectedness.

Moyers: Yet there's a lot of joy in your poems.

Lee: I hope there is. I wouldn't want to think that I write poems that make people sad.

Moyers: Your family will find themselves in your poems and in this new book, *Rose*, in particular.

Lee: Actually, I really dislike the poems in that book.

Moyers: Why?

Lee: I don't know. I think that's my father. There's the answer to your question. Nothing I do is going to be good enough for him, so everything I write I hate a week later. My poet friends tell me, "I hate the poems in my first book too, but I like the poems I'm writing now." But I hate the poems I'm *working* on. As I'm writing them, I'm realizing this is not Ecclesiastes, this is not The Song of Songs, and yet I realize I have a duty to finish those poems, and I know that they're going to help me get to the next poem.

Moyers: Why do it?

Lee: Maybe I'm obsessive by nature—my father was obsessive by nature—but it's probably really a love of a state of being. I think when a person is in deep prayer, all of that being's attention is focused on God. When a person is in love, all of that being's attention is focused on the beloved. I think in writing poetry, all of the being's attention is focused on some inner voice. I don't mean to sound mystical, but it really is a voice and all of the attention is turned toward that voice. That's such an exhilarating state to be in that it's addictive.

Moyers: It's like rapture?

Lee: Yes, a kind of rapture and a joyful sorrow and a mixture of other things as well.

Moyers: So you can't not write.

Lee: Correct. At this point in my life, I can say I can't not write. It might change, you know?

Moyers: You're thirty-one now. Are you suggesting you might not be a poet for the rest of your life?

Lee: Even now I don't consider myself a poet. I get very nervous when people say, "Oh, you're a poet." I don't feel like a poet. David, the Psalmist, was a poet. Milton was a poet. Li-po was a poet. I'm working hard to be a poet; that's the way I like to think of it.

Moyers: But if you've published a book of acclaimed poems and you're not sure you're a poet yet, how will you know when you're a poet?

Lee: I have no idea. I guess my father is going to have to materialize and tell me, "You're OK now. I think you're a poet now." I simply have the sense that I'm not there yet.

Waiting for a Final Shapeliness to Occur

Anthony Piccione and Stan Sanvel Rubin

The following conversation took place 27 February 1991 during Lee's visit to the State University of New York College at Brockport. He spoke with poets Anthony Piccione and Stan Sanvel Rubin. Printed by permission of the Brockport Writers Forum and Videotape Library.

Rubin: In the new collection, *The City in Which I Love You,* I'd like to ask you about the notion of waiting in "Here I Am" and "Waiting."

Lee: For me so much of poetry and the making of poetry have to do with a willingness to wait for something to yield itself. It's a powerlessness that one allows to occur. In my own life I feel as if I do a lot of waiting, and it seems to me a proper posture of the heart, or the mind, waiting for the poem to arrive. Or waiting for a final shapeliness to occur in my own life. Or waiting for a god to show himself. Waiting for the dead to come back.

Rubin: In a later poem you say something like "Because we have not learned not to want, we have to learn how to wait."

Lee: It has to do with desire, of course: the waiting is so fraught with desire, and longing. It's the hardest thing to do. As I said in "Here I Am," it has so little to do with patience—or even hope. Sometimes that's the whole point: to be full of longing, of desire, to be waiting.

Rubin: Does the poem sometimes come when you were waiting for something else?

Lee: I keep wondering whether or not I can realize a personal destiny. Once I begin wondering about that, I begin longing, reaching ahead, and waiting for and desiring that final form. The whole work of a human being is to try to reach that final form before one ends. And that has to do with the shapeliness in the poem, too.

Piccione: I want to ask you about the waiting which that implies, even beyond ordinary faith. What is beyond that faith?

Lee: It fluctuates, or it falls in different directions, each time. Sometimes it is a faith in an acceptance that no matter what unfolds, no matter what the shapeliness is, that it *is* right, whether it's dark or not. Somehow I have to accept that.

Piccione: What does it feel like having to accept that? Is that where the anxious energy is?

Lee: Yes, it's there, and it's full of terror. It's full of a desire and longing for the shapeliness, but a terror that the shapeliness might not be exactly what I had bargained for.

Piccione: When someone makes a great statement such as: "God, I've had enough of Your love and I'd like to break now." This isn't imitative of, say, Milton; this is a real human being in Chicago, a real city, on the third floor of his apartment, late at night, saying this. Can you talk about that a little bit? It's a very, very personal and particular relationship, isn't it?

Lee: First of all, I grew up having the Old Testament read to me continually, and when my family was wandering around in Southeast Asia, my father would translate from the Hebrew. He gave his whole life to this *God*, and the God was one who chewed us up and spit us back out and asked us to love him. The poem is a quarrel with the demands of that God, and somehow a participation. I don't think that—and when I say this, it seems so arrogant—the only task of being human is to submit to a Greater Will. Somehow I feel like we have to participate in that Greater Will: we have to bargain with him or it, or denounce it, and somehow reaffirm it by our arguments. I don't see how submitting affirms so much the existence of a Higher Power. Submission leads to complacency.

Piccione: How do you feel about being one of the few people using the word *God* in a poem? How do *you* end up being the one to use that word so comfortably, so personally?

Lee: God, I don't know . . . I . . . I . . . . It's for me an absolutely critical issue. Whether or not there is a Godliness and a sacredness in the world—everything rides on that. The stakes are so high for me. It isn't choosing between sacredness and the mundane: for me the mundane isn't even the *mundane* without the sacredness; it isn't even a thing itself. It isn't as though without the sacredness bread is just bread; the bread isn't even just bread without the sacredness. So I have to locate that sacredness. I guess at some point I just gave up and began addressing the God I grew up with.

Piccione: Just to have this go one step further, we would be hard-pressed to explain to some students that what you just said about your relationship to bread and the sacramental everywhere you look is what we *mean* when we talk about poetry. And that your poems aren't by any means *imagined,* or made up. How do we begin to talk about this real subject, in real terms? It's *you,* the solitude, it's late at night, you're writing something, and you're not making it up. I think about workshops especially, workshop poetry students, whose first instinct—and it's not their fault, either—is to *imagine,* make something up imaginatively. What do you say to that split?

Lee: I suppose that there is room for *imagined* literature, a literature written as a cultural event. I'm not sure one is better, but I know that I grew up witnessing a man for whom literature was bread. It meant getting through the next day, through the next year, a belief that countries dissolve, friends die, people get imprisoned, governments abuse you, and yet there's something else. It wasn't a polite activity; it wasn't a literary event. Unfortunately, or fortunately, I grew up reading the Old Testament as a sacred text, not as literature. Milton did not read the Bible as literature; for him it was a sacred text. Donne did not read it as literature. In a way we've lost something if we can only approach it as literature.

Rubin: Your father, we all know, was such an amazing and powerful presence throughout the collection *Rose,* and the poem "Furious Versions," that begins this collection, *The City in Which I Love You,* still has him very actively present. The collection seems a shedding of that tremendous influence, a finding of some other direction. In the poem you read, "This Hour and What Is Dead," there's a line, "Someone tell him he should sleep now." There is a poem I like very much, "My Father, in Heaven, Is Reading Out Loud," which also seems to me to be accepting the presentness of your life and in some sense trying to put some kind of final shape to that father who so dominates *Rose* and the beginning of this collection. I wonder if you'd speak about this issue which I think is simply the presence of your father in the second book.

Lee: The shedding of this influence of my father is more than changing subjects. Part of me wishes that it were that simple. But for me the writing is so personal that I have to get beyond the figure of this all-knowing, all-powerful, fierce, loving, and all-suffering figure. I have to somehow get beyond that in my own life, in order to continue, in order to achieve my own final shapeliness. Or I'll be forever contending with the existence of these fabricated character-istics of all-powerful, all-knowing, and so on. Part of me has to dismantle that in order to get through it in my own life. I guess I'm doing that in my own writing, too.

Rubin: I wonder how you put the book together. I see in my own reading this movement away from the really dominant father-figure to other things, to this moment, the next moment: is it praise or lament hidden in the next moment of your life? Did you feel consciously or later in organizing the book that you were moving to an assumption of a newer identity, or that you were looking in a different direction?

Lee: You know, I felt something very strange when I was organizing the book, a grief: while I was moving away from the figure of the father I was also moving away from the last evidence of a life I would never see again—that is, the life of the refugee and the immigrant. I feel as if I work hard to stop becoming a refugee. Part of me wants to become, of course, assimilated in America and at home. I want to feel at home here in this continent. And as I put him away, part of me realizes that what I'm putting away is this vestige of refugee and immigrant life, which has to do, of course, with old coats and rotting shoes and books falling apart and old luggage. I'm putting all of that away so that in a way I'm moving into a life that I don't really recognize. I'm leaving a life I recognize—my father, that ferocity, that consummate love for a God that devours. I see all of that and I recognize it. I know how to live under those conditions. I know how to live with the rotten luggage and the inability to speak in another person's tongue. The new thing I'm moving into, I don't recognize. When I was putting the book together, it was full of a grief as I was moving into America. I don't recognize America. I don't know how to be American—although I am, I think, ostensibly very American and assimilated. But there must be a void deep inside of me, still wandering around with his father in Macao and Singapore with all his luggage and stuff. I feel deeply attached to that.

Rubin: How many years have you been in the United States?

Lee: Let me see. I came here when I was about six, and I'm thirty-three now. What is that? About twenty-seven. That's a long time, and I can't believe how long it takes for a person to feel at home. I feel *absolutely* dislocated. Totally alienated. I didn't know that until I finished this book. I don't think I felt dislocated before because I had *him*, this great figure of the refugee that I recognized and I could identify with.

Piccione: Have you finally come to terms with your father enough to ask God to relax so you can understand him? What audacity, in fact, what wonderful audacity, you have to demand that God explain himself.

Lee: I don't see it as audacity. I feel like that's what God would want—what she or he would want. In the title poem of *The City in Which I Love You*, God is a she. I feel as if that's what our job is.

Piccione: So *personally*, when waiting for the next moment to reveal praise or lament, if you get five laments in a row instead of some other kind of blossoming, does that affect the tone or the pitch of your questioning?

Lee: It might affect the tenor or the pitch, but I don't think it affects the direction. Finally, I think all of my being's attention—I *hope*—is turned to God. If I get five laments in a row, I'm not through yet.

Piccione: Is it a matter of luck changing the tone? In fact, you've had enormous *good* luck, and your family has had an enormous long line of pretty *horrid* luck. What your father stood for, you stand for in your own way and in your own terms. And *he* would live and die by what he said and believed in, and you know that you would, too. Could you talk about that sense of luck?

Lee: When I turned thirty-three, I thought to myself, When my father was thirty-three he was thrown into jail, and I thought, God, even my suffering can't compete with that. I don't think that a human being, strangely enough, wishes only for good things; I think a human being finally wishes for the largest things . . .

Piccione: . . . or the real things.

Lee: . . . or the real things. I don't mind suffering as long as it's really about something. I don't mind great luck, if it's about something. If it's the hollow stuff, then there's no gift, one way or the other. I don't think I'm being romantic when I say that suffering occurred to a lot of people during the time of my father's imprisonment—all over the island of Java—but that suffering was *about* something. It was about human darkness. I'm not saying that makes it any *better.* All I'm saying is that I'm not trying to reduce it into a manageable thing. All a person wants is everything in its right proportion, not reduced or enlarged.

Piccione: I wish I could think of an example, but part of the change in your voice has to do with your finding yourself being the spokesman for a nation not quite awake, or a nation of sleepwalkers whose dream this also is and whose luck this also is, this kind of psychic luck that we're encountering. Your subdued, agitated ferocity, which I notice as culminating deliveries toward the end of a poem, where you say, This is what I know and it includes God, and it's this and this and this, and it's dark or it's light, but this is how it feels—that's not in *Rose,* that voice especially. You have much more opportunity in *Rose* to stay young and to stay soft. "The Weight of Sweetness" is one of my favorite poems, because it's sweetly true about a certain way of the psyche. And now you're carrying this other weight. Of course, that happened gradually. Could you tell me a little bit about how you came that way?

Lee: I don't think I ever intended, or intend, to be a spokesman. I think what happened was really very simple—not simple, maybe, but the step is a short one. As soon as a human being begins to wonder about the possibility of a personal destiny—a personal, ultimate shapeliness—that person can just lift his or her eyes half an inch and begin wondering about a kind of collective destiny, whether or not humankind has an ultimate achievement to meet with, or to attain.

It's about attainment and fulfillment so I think from the personal to the communal is just a little step.

Rubin: Can I bring that very point to the title poem, "The City in Which I Love You"? It's a tremendous poem, one of several long poems in the collection which leave me really breathless and silent. I wonder about composing such a poem in terms of what we were just saying: it's a phantasmagoria, in a sense, of all the cities of the twentieth century—the bombed-out cities, the prisoners, the tortured, all the exiles, you expand your own personal situation or history into the communal. How did you go about writing this particular poem? How did this dream/nightmare come to you, in the guise of a love poem?

Lee: I started out to write a love poem. I think there is a kind of love for a specific other, which becomes so intense that it transforms itself into a love for a greater other. You want so much to locate the core of the other that as you begin penetrating into the other you begin realizing that what you're really after is the great other in each and every one of us. I thought I was writing a poem that was sexual, a poem of longing and desire. It began to be something else. I *was* in fact wandering around a lot in Chicago, and walking through the bombed-out neighborhoods.

Rubin: How did it start? The first word of the poem is *and*. How did it first come to you? How long did it take to grow? How did you work it?

Lee: It took me a long time. I write so slowly. I think it took me about three years to write. It began as a love poem, and the more I wrote, the more desire I felt; the more desire I felt, the less fulfillment I felt, and the less fulfillment I felt, the more desire I felt and so the more I wrote. It just kept growing. I did feel as though I was trying to enter the other, to locate the other, which felt like entering a city.

Rubin: Were you surprised when this darker imagery, which is really almost hallucinatory, so intense with twentieth-century political history . . .?

Lee: Yes, I was surprised, and in the poem I keep saying, I'm not that woman, and I'm not that man. The imagination would be committing a criminal act if I said I could identify with all these people, but I know exactly what they're going through. I witnessed that as a child—the man lying there and the woman fanning his face. Now I realize that the greatest act of love I could commit is to give them their otherness, their absolute aloneness, their dignity. I don't want to go in there and muddle it up, to say, I'm just like them.

Rubin: That's an amazing moment in the poem, and it seems to be possibly the important moment for you, when you were finding your own separateness from what you identified yourself with so strongly.

Lee: Yes, because it's so easy, of course, to feel brotherly and sisterly, a love for all things and a wanting to enter them.

Rubin: At the end of the poem you come back to the city in which I love you, and you say, "I enter without retreat or help from history." There is no help from history, is there?

Lee: Right.

Rubin: Where is there help? Is it in the waiting?

Lee: I guess only in the waiting. Somehow there is a kind of faith I have in the waiting itself.

Rubin: Is that you? Who is the "you" at the end of the poem? How do you feel about the final "you"? "I re-enter the city in which I love you." Is that the particular beloved that you thought you were starting to address at the beginning, or is it a wholly expanded "you"?

Lee: I don't know.

Piccione: It has to be all of the above. Part of the question that you just asked, I was going to ask, too. We can talk about poetry and your explanation about the poem turned to your noticing something about evolutionary spiritual life which includes finding out by noticing exact particulars of your first love, finding out what otherness means. I was prompted to add, finding the way in the things of the universe, above and beyond books and words. You went to the scary place as a samurai-orphan, saying, I don't know anything, let me try again. What's it like to love the beloved? What's it like to seek God? That's what your poetry does.

Lee: I'm really moved by what you're saying, Tony, and in fact I wish it were otherwise; I wish I could have it some other way. There's a kind of dumbness about me: I feel sometimes like a dumb animal, especially when I was writing that poem. I really felt—this is very personal now—I was so full of craving I was just going out of my mind. Again it wasn't an *idea*: I didn't think, Well, I'll do this. I was just so full of craving and longing, wandering around, looking for the center of my beloved, wondering, There she was asleep in bed, but really where is she? I couldn't locate it. I was just going crazy, hungering, waiting. And a lot of the poems, I think, are about hunger, too.

Rubin: Hunger and food are important in these poems. In the process of writing this one poem, I gather you found yourself writing it over three years, while other poems were coming, complete.

Lee: Oh, yeah.

Rubin: How does it end up being essentially in these five-line stanzas? How does it achieve form? Is it coming all the time in form?

Lee: The poem did come in long lines, and I noticed that some of the lines began to cluster around five lines. That was almost a hint, and I began to look for that to occur in other places. In a way the poem gave me the clue to its own form.

Rubin: In such an intense process that this poem called forth, do you do much revising?

Lee: Yeah, I think during the three years most of it was cutting and revising. It was originally about forty pages and I cut it down to what it is in the book. It feels like it wants to be longer and then shorter. It feels ragged to me.

Piccione: Your poems are getting longer. How do you account for that?

Lee: Because I am so in love with the attention of the poetic moment that I just want it to go on.

Rubin: When do you write best? When is your most receptive moment?

Lee: I think when the kids are asleep. Usually at night. I work from about nine at night to five in the morning.

Piccione: You said something before that I'm going to add to my definition of what I mean by "poet": any poet, good or bad, must be called a "craver."

Lee: Yeah, it seems to me that desire, longing, craving, hunger—without it there's no urgency, or impetus.

Piccione: And your good luck is that you're a slow learner, and so you slowly, patiently, carefully look at each thing. What about that attention to form? And part of your attention has to be the public attention *you* receive. Do you start thinking, What does it look like? How will it be received? Is this clear to nearly everyone? Is that entering more and more your editing consciousness?

Lee: No.

Piccione: So it's not a great danger for you.

Lee: I don't think so. I don't think I've ever taken that into consideration at all.

Rubin: When you were talking about becoming an American as an ongoing process, you said you were alienated and hadn't fully realized it. Would you speak about this alienation?

Lee: I should say first of all that one of the things I'm beginning to discover is that this alienation is *not* all bad. It's a gift, in a way. My *otherness*, though I've spent years being pained and anxious about it, finally is a gift. Finally, we *are* all other to each other. It's not a *sweet* gift, necessarily, but it *is* true. And again as long as it's true I don't want to reduce or enlarge it. It *is* something; it isn't hollow.

Piccione: That's what set you out trying to overcome it in the first place, right?

Lee: Right! Right! Exactly! That was it absolutely there, and it's all attached. It has to do with the way I sit inside my body, that growing up, looking like the other, made the others around me treat me like the other, and so I began to feel like the other, the foreigner, the alien, and it's very simple if you have that physically impressed upon you, then you *are* trapped inside this body so everywhere you go you do feel like you are the other.

Piccione: Everybody else has that. I think you're on to something.

Rubin: It's almost a definition of America you're offering, in a way: I suppose multiculturalism, which is much talked about in education and art, really means everyone acknowledging everyone else's otherness, which you do in "The City in Which I Love You." Along this line I'd like to come to the final poem, "The Cleaving," in which you come back to your face, opening and closing the book with your own face.

Lee: The poem was a little terrifying to write because finally in order to see everybody in myself and to see myself in everyone else I had to do violence to myself. I don't think it was transcendent in the way one normally thinks of transcendence. I used to think of transcendence as easy, light, full of wings, or something like that. I realized there's only one kind of transcendence, a kind of violence, because I think living in America is a violent experience, especially if you do feel like the other. And I think assimilation is a *violent* experience. One of violence's names is change.

Rubin: This is literally a very bloody imagery—butchering—and it's an imagery of eating really wonderful food. It's a vision of being consumed and consuming. That seems to me the opposite of transcendence on some level.

Lee: Right, but it's also a way of becoming attached to humanity, but it comes through a kind of imminence.

Rubin: But you're also accepting death in some way, participating in it.

Piccione: How *do* we end up? Do we win in this, or not?

Lee: That's the other thing when I was writing the poem. I came to the realization that poetry isn't pretty or nice. It's very hard, when we talk about being obsessed or consumed.

Piccione: In order for the light and sweetness to remain real you have to go here, too.

Lee: I think you have to.

Art Is Who We Are

Patty Cooper and Alex Yu

The following conversation took place in February 1996 in the Lee household which includes Li-Young's wife and children as well as his brother Li-Lin, his wife and children. Li-Young's wife Donna and Li-Lin's wife Denise are sisters. The interview appeared in Riksha *in early 1997. Reprinted by permission.*

Cooper: Dwight [Okita] said you threw away three drafts before sending in a final draft [of *The Winged Seed*].

LYL: Three? More like a hundred. I was writing like a book a week. It was an impossible problem I set for myself. It's going to have to contain some narrative and has to have some length. Somehow it has to accomplish the feeling that the book was an instant in time—one instant—the way a lyric poem is. The poem is an instant of seeing, and I wanted the book to have the feel as though it was just a flash. I didn't know how I was going to accomplish that except that I would have to sit down and see if I could write the book in one night.

Cooper: Is that why you threw away so many copies, because it was a moment and then you had to create another moment?

LYL: Yes, because some of those moments were more coherent than others, some moments better than other moments. Near the end my lovely editor—I was sending him like a book a week! He was going out of his mind. He was calling the agent saying, "What is this guy? What is he doing? Why is this stuff showing up on my desk every week? A new book and they're all different?" And then I told him I'm writing a book a week and I thought I would write the book in one night. Needless to say, I couldn't do it. So I would sit down and try to write it. But every night I would sit down and think, This is it, I'm going to write the book tonight. I did that for five years. Finally, I got it down to three nights. So I was writing a book in three nights and another book in three nights and another book in three nights.

Yu: What's going to happen to the others then?

LYL: Well, they're just sitting there.

Yu: Any possibility for publishing later on?

LYL: I don't think so. I'll be honest with you, I feel a little bereft because they took the book out of my hands saying, "This is good, this is going to be published."

Cooper: Are they calling it your biography?

LYL: No, a remembrance. I wanted to write a poem, a prose poem, not even a prose poem, but a poem, and that was an interesting challenge for me, to try to write a poem in one night, two hundred pages, very long lines, the whole thing was just so crazy. Because ultimately, to be quite honest with you, I don't have a lot of respect for prose.

Cooper: You don't? That hurts.

LYL: I do. I have a little respect for prose. I just feel as if poetry is the language itself and that in prose the language is doing something else.

Cooper: Poetry is your language, right. Is that what you're saying?

LYL: No, I'm talking about the condition of language in prose that you use language to talk about something. But in poetry, you're being used by language. Language is the master in poetry, it masters you. But in prose, it feels to me, you master the language in order to talk about something else.

Yu: There was a piece of work you [Li-Lin] did called *Golden Seed.* Does that have any relation to *The Winged Seed?*

LLL: Just both our drunkenness. No, there's no conscious attempt. There may be an unconscious [relation], but I don't know.

Yu: There are similarities in your work that are very interesting. For instance, the layering that you both do in paint and in words. Did you notice that in yourselves?

LLL: I never noticed that our work had any similarities, to tell you the truth. Except that maybe we talk about the same things, but not in the work, you know what I mean? So that's interesting to hear that you see these similarities.

Cooper: How was it when you guys worked on that project together that you showcased at the Walsh Gallery? About the process—how did that go?

LLL: That was really interesting. In fact, we're trying to do another project with a publisher of that type of collaboration. We thought about different approaches. One was that he would just write a poem and I would do a little visual to accompany the poem. And then we thought, Well, that was kind of not interesting. Then we thought about actually visualizing the poem as well, in other words, visualizing his half of it as well as my half. So we finally got it down to where he was basically writing his rough drafts on paper, then we would actually take the rough drafts and cut them up and they would be part of the work so it would be a totally visual experience. It was a really free thing. But a lot of people were saying, 'Well, I can't read the poem.' It's like, You're not supposed to read the poem. It's supposed to be a visual thing. It's not supposed to be a visual thing where you read the poem and look at the picture. In our next project we might actually have the poem readable and then have the visual somehow incorporated into it.

Yu: In the book, *The Transforming Visions*, you [Li-Lin] already had your piece in the collection [at the Art Institute of Chicago], so you [Li-Young] had to put the poem together especially for the book. How did you go about doing that?

LYL: Well, I just looked at the work and I knew I didn't want to write a poem to describe it. I wanted to do what I thought the work was doing. And so to my mind, when I looked at it, it was paneled. So it had a feeling of seriality to it, like there were many rooms in a larger room. It was non-representational, but there was a richness to it. It seemed to refer, possibly, to an interior. So I just took that and I thought, Well, let's see if I could write a poem that was serial, have a feeling of many rooms; at the same time, it seems to refer to a human interior that isn't recognizable—a new human interior—and so that was a challenge for me to write the poem.

Yu: You relate things to architecture. I remember you talking once about a piece of architecture reminding you of this or that as a memory play.

LYL: Oh, no, that wasn't for that piece. For instance, I would notice that the piece, his painting, had no center to it and at the same time there's no circumference to it. So I knew I had to write a poem in which there was no center and no circumference. It seemed to refer infinitely beyond itself and at the same time it had a cohesiveness to it. It wasn't just random, although it looks almost random. In other words, it's a picture of the universe. When you try to describe the painting, what you come up with is a picture of the universe. There's no center, the circumference is everywhere.

Yu: It's funny you say that because another similarity in both your work, I think, is that there's a focus, yet it's still very opaque, very diffused. Does either of you see that in both your work?

LLL: For me it was always one of the aspects of Chinese landscape painting. How there's never a focus or a center but many foci and many centers. That probably had the biggest effect on me and my work. I don't like to think of things in that way—just one focus—but of many things, a myriad of things. That always interested me.

Yu: What Li-Young saw in your piece, *Corban Ephphatha I,* was that the same kind of thoughts you had when you created the piece? That was back in 1992?

LLL: Around '91, '92. I wasn't thinking of it in that clear of terms. I was just working with approximations. At the time I was reading a book Li-Young gave me, a translation of the Greek New Testament. Not that the work was about the book or anything like that. It just happened as I was doing the work I was reading that book. So there was a certain sense of connection in my thoughts and in my ideas about life, about myself. I think I was also explaining in my work spirituality and exploring the connection between our physical body or physical needs, where those physical aspects meet the spiritual aspects because painting is such a physical thing, but at the same time you're trying to take it beyond that. But ultimately in your work, you're working with this substance called paint. So I was very much involved with that state of mind, of how the physical can become spiritual and vice versa because Christianity denies the physical. It's like,You feel something? No, it's not there. Deny everything. Deny all your feelings. Deny all your bodily functions. Which I don't agree with. There has to be some kind of union between the two—the physical and the spiritual. So that's why I chose the title because "Corban" means "Gift of God" and "Ephphatha" was the term that Jesus used when he was healing. He would say "Ephphatha" which is "to be open."

Cooper: Yet it seems the Christian faith is not.

LYL: Well, not the way we have it. It's lost its mystical ground, like the Thomas gospel, and we don't know anything about those. In fact, if you read the New Testament and the Old Testament, if you could read it purely, without all the stuff we're told it means, it's a very sensual text. It's just pure, beautiful, spiritual sensuality. The women anointing, shattering the alabaster, all of that stuff, washing the feet, turning of water into wine—all of that is sensuality. And they forgot it started out as a slave religion, a religion of outcasts and outsiders. It's lost its connection to mystical ground. It is basically a mystical religion. That's what religion is.

Yu: What kind of lasting effect did your father, being a minister, have on both of you?

LLL: We were both very religious as young boys. We still are, but maybe in a more universal way. We were almost fanatic. We studied the Bible a lot. My father is an interesting influence because he was very scholarly in his approach to religion, and yet at the same time he had an extremely passionate and personal relationship with his God. So we, being bi-cultural, [our father] was also able to bring in a lot of the Chinese spiritual understandings. There was a strange mix, almost like Christianity through Taoism, or something like that. I think we were able to get a bigger picture of what spirituality means through my father.

Yu: I think there's a lot of that going around where there's a mesh of the two.

LLL: Now there are. But when we were growing up, it was [different], plus we grew up in an all-white community, very WASPy.

Cooper: How do you feel about that?

LLL: Alone. Alienated, basically.

Cooper: Does that affect you now? I mean, the place of Asian Americans today?

LYL: Well, that's so strange because when we were growing up, Asian Americans we knew wanted nothing to do with us. On the one hand, we would meet them and the ones who were born here felt we were too Chinese because we were very traditional, but the ones who were not born here felt we were too Western. The Asian-American community wasn't a refuge for us. So it wasn't the experience that people have on the West Coast—the refuge and the real satisfaction of ideas, where people share like things. It wasn't like that. We were really outside. I mean, outside white culture, outside Asian-American culture. Outside. You know, just outside.

Cooper: How do you feel now?

LYL: Outside.

Cooper: You've got the whole family in the building. That's all you need.

LYL: Yes, exactly. We were so outside that we thought, Well, it gets pretty cold and lonely, so at least we'll just be all together and be outside this way. That's the way it always felt to me. Did it feel that way to you [Li- Lin]?

LLL: But at the same time I always believed we've actually managed to totally assimilate American culture, and totally retain our Chinese heritage. I was just looking through this [*Riksha*], there was a little blurb in there about somebody saying that being American [the author who was Korean was adopted at a very young age] meant hating himself for being Korean. But that was never actually a thing, at least for me, and I think it's that way with all of us. In those years growing up, we were out there. You know, running around, playing with the white kids, playing at their houses and just being normal American kids, then we'd come home and speak Mandarin and eat

Chinese food. There was never any, at least for me, feeling of conflict. It was always just total wonderment. Oh, this is what's happening. Like, Wow!

Yu: It's hard for me to believe there was no racism.

LLL: That's why it was kind of a shock for me whenever I would meet—I remember as a young child—I would meet certain Asian-American kids who were really heavily into denial. I still meet them. I would meet adults who are those kids grown up. They're heavily into denial of their heritage, but at the same time I can kind of see that they've not assimilated into American culture either. Because the true American culture is not a denial of your own heritage, but is a contribution of your heritage into the American, you know, American whatever. In a way I think there might be a danger with what's happening right now with this delineation of Asian-American art or Asian-American literature. We might be in danger of ghettoizing ourselves, into some little category that might be easily manipulated by the white culture. Once they've got you all penned up, they turn you around in their hands and toss you over. I think there's an important aspect about us as Asian Americans that we must share ourselves with everyone. That's the main thing—to share.

Yu: I think there's some Asian-American artists out there that don't like associating with the Asian-American groups just because they don't want to get that stigma.

LLL: It's such a very complicated issue. To me there must be involvement. Asian Americans got to stick together. But at the same time we have to be careful not to get ourselves all corralled. So I don't agree with those people who don't want to be involved either. That's also a mistake because that makes us weak.

Cooper: So do you feel that way, Li-Young?

LYL: I do. And I feel that more than ever. It's a hard thing to juggle. When they introduce Philip Levine to do a reading, they don't say, "Here's the Jewish-American poet, Philip Levine." They just say "the American poet." When they introduce me, they say, "He's the Chinese-American poet."

Cooper: And he's escaped from here and been through here and made it to America.

LLL: [*Singing*] Born in a chicken coop . . .

LYL: As a poet, you just want to be known as a poet. You want to be shoulder to shoulder with Whitman, Dickinson, and all the other poets. If an artist thinks of himself as an Asian-American artist, if it's a term of empowerment, then we should use it. But if people are saying, Well, these are the poets, and those are the minority poets— that bothers me.

Cooper: I look at your work, it's about family, spirituality, being lonely, afraid. Those are things every person in the world has felt, and if they say they haven't, they're a liar.

LLL: That's another thing: that a lot of art by Asian Americans is about being Asian-American. That's a very dangerous thing because that's supposing that there's something unusual about us. There may be certain things about us that are unique, but ultimately all our experiences are universal. We have to transcend, especially in art what I call trivial aspects of our existence and move on to greater issues. That's really what art is all about, not this momentary thing, like AIDS. It's like, "I'm going to write all these poems or paint all these paintings about AIDS." AIDS is a real thing. It's very frightening. It's very important in our time. But at the same time, is it art?

Cooper: We were talking about your father. I know that your work, Li-Young, has been affected a lot by your father. In your new book, are you still exploring that?

LYL: Yes, my work has always been a struggle between the personal and impersonal. It's always been an impersonal voice I'd like to achieve. I'll be honest with you, every poem, at the risk of oversimplifying, is at least about two things. There's this subject, in this case let's say the father, and then the poem is about itself. The poem, if it's successful, enacts its own making. That's what we mean when we say in the best light, poetry is about poetry. The poem is like a person. You are about your history. You're referential in that you refer to yourself. You're about your parents, where you come from, but you're also about you and a poem is like that.

The making of every poem is new, and the freshness of every poem comes from the skill or the luck of whether or not the poet can enact a new kind of making in each poem. Though the subject is the father, the making of the poem for me is from scratch. My hope is that the poem is always different somehow because each making is a new making and so each poem is different in the way it solves a musical quandary. That's basically what a poem does: it solves musical problems. When I say musical problems, I mean problems of voice, of tone, language, rhythm—that kind of thing.

The whole thing is self-enclosed because the poem sets up its own quandaries and solves them. In a way it doesn't refer to anything outside of itself. Like if you read a really wonderful poem, you can't get that experience somewhere else. So let's say you read a great Frost poem, or you read a great Li-po poem about the mountains in Su Jo, you really can't go to Su Jo and have the same experience as reading the poem. You might think you could and say after reading this poem, "I have to go see those mountains."

A lot of this new book is about my father. It's almost too easy because a lot of times a person thinks, I'll write about something instead of my father. I'll write about horses. But the musical quandary is the same. They've changed the subjects, but their solutions are the same solutions, so they've just merely changed subjects and you're actually looking at the same poem. A person can actually have the same subject the rest of his life, all of his or her life, but the poems are different somehow. Somebody like Roethke, he only had two: love and death. Let me say this, there are only two subjects: love and death. Everything else is the dross.

Yu: Is it love and death or life and death?

LYL: I would say love and death because love is life. Death is either negation or fertility depending on how you solve that quandary each time. When you write a poem, basically you have a stage: you put a little tree here, a little house here, and you watch love and death enact and as you wipe that out, you put a little coastline here and you watch love and death enact there, but it's the same subject.

Cooper: Is that the mystery? You're writing a mystery every single time.

LYL: Absolutely. Did you ever read a poet and get bored with him so you think, Well . . . A lot of times what's boring is his musical solutions are all the same. It's not his subject matter, it's his musical solutions. If you are somebody like Tu Fu or Li-po, the great ones, like Dickinson, every poem was a new experience. It was a new problem, and they had to have new solutions for that linguistic problem and that's what freshness is.

Yu: Do you [Li-Lin] use the same kind of methodology?

LLL: No, not really. My approach is not a literary approach to art.

Yu: There's a problematic solution to it: the paint is like the words and the theme is subject. It's solving a problem and having the same subjects.

LLL: For me it's the very opposite, because the very act of painting is the act of the manipulation of material and trying to make that material mean something. It's almost like it's automatically vague— a losing proposition. You never finish a painting, you never solve a problem; you only wind up bringing more questions, bringing up more problems.

Yu: Questions in theme or . . .

LLL: Formal questions, questions of composition, but more importantly questions of life. When you look at a painting that clearly communicates something, that's not really about the paint. That's about using the paint to do something. It's kind of like prose, using the paint to paint a picture of something. But when you're being used by the paint, you wind up asking more questions, even questioning your own purposes. Why are you even doing this? What's the point?

Yu: Don't you [Li-Young] come up with questions afterward, after you complete a poem, or do you think there's a finality to it?

LYL: No, a lot of times the solution is irresolution. The poem ends open-ended.

Yu: So there are questions brought up in the same way he has questions brought up, but aren't there solutions in the formality of the painting?

LLL: Well, hopefully no. When I see a great painting, the first thing that goes on in my head is, Man, this doesn't make any sense, but it feels wonderful.

Yu: So it's the irrational speaking to you, not the rational.

LLL: It's irrational in a logical sense, but it's totally rational in an internal sense. When you look at something and you understand and love it, but at the same time, in here [*pointing to his head*] it doesn't make any sense to me at all.

LYL: See, that's what I would call a visceral resolution because a lot of the time a poem commits a visceral resolution but not an intellectual one. Intellectually it's like, Where does that leave us? That we're all doomed? That the world is coming to an end? But viscerally it's like, Wow, that was musically satisfying. It isn't enough for me to go into the project to say, "Well, there's no resolution, but I'm just going to do it." Because the stakes are so low for me. That's like saying, "Let's go on a search for the Grail. We all know there's no such thing as the Grail, but let's drive a yellow bus across the United States and act nutty." That's not enough for me. The stakes have to be, "I heard there's a Grail, I'm going to find it even though it means I never do." The stakes go up. For me, poetry is a play for mortal stakes. It's a great play of language. It's pleasure, but for mortal stakes. If I thought for one second that, No, it's all irresolution, it's all random, I wouldn't do it. I have to believe there is something even though every time I'm finished I come up with nothing. I come up with these really dark to open-ended irresolutions. That's OK, but I know that I was sincere about trying to find a resolution.

Yu: Do you feel closer to that resolution after each one, or do you feel farther, or a little bit of both?

LYL: My experience is that when I'm done writing a poem, the knowledge that it took to write that poem doesn't help me write the next one. So the next one, I start from scratch. I'm no closer to any resolution. I start in a quandary. But sometimes I end up in a quandary, but not because I believe that's where we are, but that's where I actually ended up.

LLL: I think there's a danger to always comparing painting and literature because they're so different. Clement Greenberg said, "Ultimately, painting is about fashion." Just color alone is so connected to vanity and to fashion that we can't get away from it. There are certain things inherent in painting that don't exist at all in literature.

Cooper: Is that what attracts you?

LLL: Yes. I've always been attracted to the physical things, and that's probably why I'm a painter. In literature there's more of the intellectual. In literature, especially in poetry, there's a much higher level of communication. In painting, it's the lowest level. It's like when you see a rock cliff. You're astounded by it—the formations on this rock. That's a very low level of communication. You see it and it affects you.

Cooper: But that's instant communication, right?

LLL: Right. I always think that the poets are the angels and painters are like moles under ground, but they know that somewhere up there are angels. That's always been my feeling because painting by its pure definition is always rooted in the earth. It's so attached to vanity, to fashion. That's why a guy like Andy Warhol can be famous and respected and influential and great because of what art is to begin with. But a guy like Andy Warhol could never make it in poetry because he's too damn shallow.

Yu: So you're saying he's like hamburger for the masses.

LYL: So art is hamburger for the masses?

LLL: No, what I'm saying is there are certain things inherent in painting that is so attached to our world—painting is very worldly. The very act of manipulating this substance is a very worldly thing and the things you go through while you're painting are very worldly considerations. Choices of composition, color, blah, blah, blah, this and that. They're very worldly considerations. Poetry is otherworldly.

LYL: I think there are really worldly poets.

Yu: I think there's a heavenliness to some pieces, too.

LLL: It can evoke spirituality. I'm not saying painting can't. It's just like when you watch a belly dancer. You're watching this being shaking her belly; you can be evoked into a spiritual revelation. I remember in college we used to go to these places. This belly dancer, every time it was her day, we'd all flock over there and watch her. You could really learn something.

LYL: Feel the music through the spheres.

Cooper: That was otherworldly, right?

LLL: Yes.

Cooper: But in what region of your body was it otherworldly?

LYL: Netherworldly.

LLL: So that's how painting works for me. It's like watching this grotesque thing. Through some transformation we're seeing some spiritual gift.

Cooper: So being originally a biochemist, how does that happen? Now you're talking about spirituality, vanity, maybe that was always there. How did you make the decision?

LLL: It was a decision I made after I moved to Chicago. A friend of ours invited us to go out to some galleries. We really enjoyed it. I thought, Wow, that's amazing! So we started looking at more art, and that's when I realized this is really what I was meant to do.

Yu: What were the first paintings you saw?

LLL: I remember really getting amazed when I first saw a Brice Marden painting. He's a minimalist painter. What amazed me about his painting was that it was totally new to me. It was something I didn't understand at all. To be an adult and run into something that you totally don't understand is exciting. You want to figure out why did this guy do this.

Yu: Did you ever try to get a painting done in one night?

LLL: That idea actually sounds very attractive. My brother in New York is involved in that process.

Cooper: How many brothers and sisters are in the family?

LLL: There's four brothers and one sister.

Cooper: And everyone is an artist?

LYL: My sister is doing a libretto for the Minnesota Opera. Eric Simmons is the director.

Cooper: And your other two brothers are . . .

LLL: My oldest brother designs fashion jewelry, and my youngest is a painter also.

Yu: What do you attribute to that?

LYL: We're stupid.

LLL: We don't know any better. I'm sure my mother frequently asks herself that question. I think that's the way my parents raised us. They may disagree with that. We used to spend a lot of time gathering around the dining room table painting, drawing. My dad would be at the head of the table doing his paintings, and we would all be around doing our paintings. He'd walk around, watch what we were doing, and correct us. Every time he had a vacation, for that month all we did was paint. Or he'd pull out his accordion we'd all get little sticks and we'd all sing and make music together. Art was very much part of our lives. And I think that's why we all became artists. It was like that was our comfort. It was a thing that represented liberation and stability.

LYL: It was an essential part of our lives. You know there was food and there was sleep and there was the singing and the painting. Our first experience of art wasn't in a museum.

Yu: What did Mom and Dad say when you said, "I'm going to be a poet, I'm going to be a painter"?

LLL: My father had already passed away when I made that choice, but my mother wasn't too happy about it. She just said, "What are you going to do for a job?" I even felt that way too because I never knew that painting was something that people actually pursued with their whole life. It wasn't until I came to Chicago, I realized, Wow, this is a real thing. I just told my mother, I'm going to paint for a job, that's my job, that's my life. My father-in-law was even worse. He said, "You can't do that. How do you do that? Nobody paints, nobody draws. What are you going to do, doodle at home and that's your job?"

Cooper: [*To Li-Young*] You've dedicated all of your work to your wife. Your love for her must be incredible.

LYL: I do feel a lot of love for her. There are difficulties in relationships. I hope the new book enacts it more than the other books, this problem—I don't want to call it a problem. Well, it is a problem for me. It's an inability to make contact with a person. The body of language and the body of another person present the same challenge.

Cooper: That's interesting because a lot of people who review your work say there's an intimacy in it, and yet you say there's a place where you can't reach that intimacy.

LYL: Right. On another level it's kind of like she and people in general are a perpetual undiscovered country to me. In the same way language is. My hope in *The Winged Seed*, in the remembrance . . . is that I could enact that in the language. That the language itself could enact my inability to find a . . . I'm saying this very badly because for me it's not easy to understand. It's not very clear to me that this woman, who happens to be my wife, that the more I know her the more her boundaries . . . there are no boundaries. So I can't find where the country ends. So that's the way I experience language, too, but I can't find the boundaries of the language.

Cooper: Do you want to find the boundary?

LYL: I want to find the ground.

Cooper: Are you floating on top of it now, or you can't get in the door, or what?

LYL: No, it's more like insatiability. I don't know what satisfaction is. What's enough?

Cooper: What's enough woman or what's enough . . .

LYL: Yes, what's enough poem, what's enough woman, what's enough body, what's enough physical love, what's enough emotional love? It's never enough.

Cooper: So you're always hungry.

LYL: Yes, exactly. It's about hunger, that's what it is. My hope is that this third book enacts hunger. I hope that somehow the passages constantly enact more and more hunger.

Cooper: Does it surprise you when people say there's intimacy within your work?

LYL: No, because I do want that intimacy, but it's not intimate enough for me. I want something so intimate that it's less than whispered. I would like to reach some sort of anonymous center in me and speak from that center. My imagination tells me that voice from that center would be so intimate it would speak to everybody. It would be universal.

Cooper: This is totally off the subject, but I wanted to ask you [Li-Young] about it. Dwight told me about an experience in New York where they had asked you to read an essay about poetry.

LYL: Oh, yes.

Cooper: And you went into a seizure as you were reading this essay and to calm yourself down you read poetry. They reviewed it the next day and said, "What a brilliant performance artist."

LYL: It was in Rochester. Rochester had this hoity-toity thing called Rochester Artist Lectures—a bunch of wealthy people put out money and every month they have a writer come in and give a talk and meet the writer. They asked me to give a talk, and I said no. I said I'd come give a reading and talk a little bit about the poems. They said, "No, we would like more talk, like a lecture." I said, "No, I don't want to do that." They kept asking me. "I don't want to do that, I don't want to write a lecture." They said, "You could intersperse with poems." They kept asking me to do it. So I said, "Fine." So I went there. My talk was about how you can't talk about poetry, and I went into this seizure. My tongue got real thick and stiff in my mouth, and I couldn't move. I was ready to pass out, my right arm started to shake, my legs were starting to shake. I think all the blood dropped out of my head. I must have been like a ghost. I was ready to fall over and somebody grabbed a chair and I sat down. I couldn't talk, I was literally "thuu, thuu, thuu, thuu" like that. Somebody in the audience said, "Read a poem." So I opened a book and started reading a poem, and I was fine. I just don't like talking and there was a thousand people there. That was daunting.

LLL: You weren't feeling too well.

LYL: I was real sick. I'd taken all this medication. After that poets in the audience said, "You really proved yourself today; that was a good thing. That you couldn't do it, that was a good thing." Everyone else was baffled: What the hell was that? It was so unnerving.

Cooper: Did you try resuming the essay or did you just read poetry for the rest of the time?

LYL: No, I tried. I couldn't collect my thoughts. My head was woozy. People's voices were like echoes. People would ask questions. I would try to answer them. It was the longest hour of my life. I was really worried. It was really scary. After I had the brain scans the doctor said, "There are peaks in your [EEG] that only exist in nine-year-olds." I must have a nine-year-old's brain.

Yu: To change the subject, Li-Lin, how much editing do you do on Li-Young's books?

LLL: I'm not capable of critiquing his work, simply because I'm not literary.

Yu: You don't even look at it?

LLL: I read it and give my opinion, but I don't feel I'm qualified. With painting you don't have to be qualified. A lot of art critics don't have any background, and they're writing in major magazines. I must say some of them are actually good critics, but the thing with art is that it's less about education. Anyone can look at a painting and make an assessment; with literature it's different. It's very dangerous for a person to pretend he or she is literary and expound on an opinion when you aren't qualified.

Cooper: It doesn't seem like you think very much of art.

LLL: I do think a great deal of art when it's great. Because of the very nature of what it is I think it has that side to it. It has that real dark, seedy side to it.

LYL: I think it has to do with the artist and the poet. A poet like Rilke comes along, and suddenly the German language becomes the language of spiritual expression. That's what a really profound artist does: He comes into the field, whatever field it is, and he says, "This could be this, instead of that." Whitman comes along and turns the American language into what he turned it into. That's a possibility. If a poet wants to go into poetry and turn it into what Maya Angelou does, then that's what it is for her—that kind of easy, sappy, ready-made expression of whatever. I don't think it's the field. I think an artist can go into the art field and say, "No, it has nothing to do with fashion or vanity, it has to do with what brother van Gogh was talking about in his letters. It has to do with expression of luminosity in the universe. It has to do with the expression of sacredness in nature." And that's what he turns it into. Somebody like Jeff Koons goes into it and says, "No, it's about vanity and fashion." Who we are is what we make of the thing.

Yu: Why did you choose Chicago to be your home as opposed to the coasts where it might be more beneficial to your careers?

LYL: Our sister was here.

LLL: She actually brought us out here after college. We came out here and it was nice. It was livable. New York was just too hard to live in and L.A., who the hell wants to live in L.A.? Chicago was beautiful, very accessible. I remember we just loved Chinatown. My wife and I used to go to Chinatown almost five times a week to eat when we first moved out here. We couldn't get enough of the stuff. It's so good. New York Chinatown is such a pain in the ass to live in; you can't drive over there. It's just hard. Chicago is just so livable. It's a large city with all the amenities of a large city and it's so accessible.

Cooper: What is your advice to young Asian-Americans out there who are or want to be writers or poets or artists or painters?

LLL: Don't think of yourself as making Asian-American art; just think of yourself as making art and always remember that you are Asian-American.

LYL: If you don't have to write poetry, don't do it, unless you feel like you really have to. Because at some point it's the work itself that feeds you and sustains you and justifies you.

Cooper: You know Alex and I were going over questions to ask you. He said, "Well, should I ask them why they became artists?" And I said,

"There is no choice. You do it."

LYL: William Stafford has a great answer for that. Someone asked him, "When did you start writing poetry?" He said, "Well, I just never stopped. The rest of the world, everybody does creative things up to a point and then they quit. I just didn't quit."

Art and the Deeper Silence

Reamy Jansen

The following conversation took place in April 1996 at Li-Young Lee's home in Chicago. Printed by permission of Reamy Jansen.

>︵︵✕

Jansen: How does the notion of "testament" figure into your work?

Lee: I was interested in *The Winged Seed* in the idea of an old testament, a new testament, and that each of us somehow has to write a current testament. That's the injunction that I heard to write our own myth.

Jansen: I also hear so much of Eliot in *The City in Which I Love You,* and especially in "The Cleaving," its concluding section. I hear certain cadences, and also there's that sense of the sojourner, who, in your words, "tunnels the night."

Lee: Eliot meant a lot to me. I felt like Eliot heard something really big, and I wanted to hear something that big. I didn't want to hear what he heard; I wanted to hear something that big. I think both of us were up to the same thing. His subject is . . . the soul? Or the true soul? Maybe the soul in the condition of truth? It's interesting that his version of the true self is still wearing a lot of Christian garb. It's pretty handsome on Eliot; it's not tacky. I don't know why, but it's tacky to me on Lowell. Lowell somehow wears his Christianity badly. It's more sparing on Eliot. He's very elegant. So the poet is for me the right writing of poetry. It's the practice of what, ecstasy? Then a line of poetry, or a sentence, is an ecstatic act. But when we live in the big mind, it is always an ecstatic act. That's what it comes down to. Practice of the big mind is the practice of ecstasy. The practice of art is the practice of ecstasy. In Emerson, all of his sentences—that's why people sometimes say his essays don't make sense—he speaks out of, towards, mystery.

Jansen: They're not wholes in a conventional sense?

Lee: Yes, the mind he's using, I think, in the writing of those sentences. He's writing, if one can imagine, a 360-degree sentence. That's really hard to do. Each of his sentences, and each of his essays, is a proposition about universe mind.

Jansen: A 360 degrees that we can only apprehend with 110 degrees of sight?

Lee: Yes. Like Dante. Not the Dante of the *Inferno*, but in the *Paradiso* he does it. Unless I'm reading the *Inferno* wrong. I found the *Inferno* rumor-mongering, gossip. The *Paradiso* was more serious—artistically higher, less self-interested—and it was purer. That's the difficulty for me, right now—living in the universe mind, acting out of the universe mind, and writing out of that mind. What does it mean to do that? And what does that sound like? It would sound like Emerson, like Whitman, like Dickinson's richest stuff. It would sound like Blake . . . Christ. Like St. John of the Cross. All the ones we love. It would sound like that.

Jansen: You know, I'm also thinking of how your father created, of that elaborate paper model your father worked on and took with him, could pack and unpack everywhere your family went.

Lee: Of Solomon's Temple. That was an incredible thing he made. First of all, he represented his capacity for play, even in exile. I think that's why we're artists. [Lee's three brothers are artists; his sister is a composer]. We like to play, that's what we do. Do you know that Mayan myth, the Popol Vuh? There's these thirteen warriors, they're playing with this ball, and there's these thirteen lords of death underground who hear the ball being rolled around. They say, "Who is that?" And they tell them to come down to play. So these thirteen athletes have to play these thirteen lords of death. Sometimes I think that's what art is for the artist. You take your thirteen personalities, whoever they are, and then they play thirteen lords of death. You know, you only have two subjects, love, and death. The line of poetry actually enacts love, but somehow the margin enacts death. So it's you against the margin all the time. The stakes go up, when that's what you're doing.

It all has to do with worrying the language down into something. When I was writing *The Winged Seed*, I was hoping somehow that the book was the temple, and that, with that temple, there would be a temple within a temple, within a temple. The whole thing was like a rose. That's my model all the time, of the within that is within the within, within the within. So the poem is an infinity-inward flowering. I'm at a point now where I don't even believe that there is such a thing as an outer life . . . so that the voice of poetry is basically an infinitely inward voice.

Jansen: The language of the Bible must have been very much a voice with you as a child?

Lee: Yes, and the impression that language was the language of the ecstatic. We didn't know what that meant at the time, but we knew that when we were listening to those books being read by my father we were no longer in the ordinary. There was a practice of the extraordinary just by listening to my father read, say, the Psalms or one of the Epistles. So that was important in my life, that there was a thing called the extraordinary.

Jansen: Such as in The Book of Exodus? Rather like living in magical realism?

Lee: It was somebody telling my story in code. And why was it in code? Because that's a tradition of secrets. In all the books of the Bible there are secrets; that's part of their authority. Poetry's authority also comes from that mystery.

Jansen: The notion of "meaning," say, doesn't mean too much to you?

Lee: The meaning is a felt experience, not an understood experience. Here's the difference: I read with my whole body, so I hear a word like "ambidextrous" differently from a word like "rut." One is polysyllabic, cerebral, and Latinate; one is Germanic, monosyllabic, and highly stressed. I don't read them the same way, so I hear the language with my whole body. It's not just your mind. I know that there's really good poetry, but it feels to me that it's written by a mentality. It's very good, but I don't think it's whole. Not whole enough . . . a lot of Dickinson is like that.

Jansen: Is there, then, a tradition that lines up for you, that speaks to you in a certain way?

Lee: Whitman, Emerson, Rilke. The meaning of the Book of Exodus to me has little to do with the Israeli state. The meaning of that book has everything to do with my estate, and my soul's estate, what it means to take a personality that is many voiced, and manifold, and out of control, and to make it whole. That to me is my story; it's not just the story of its people. So I'm reading everything on a mythic scale, and, when you read everything on a mythic scale, not everything stands up to that.

Jansen: There's really a great deal of touching in your poetry. As one of the ways we know?

Lee: Maybe that's the subject? Touching and not being able to touch anything? You know what I mean? You're touching, let's say, your wife's body, a woman that you really love and the more you touch that person, the less that person's there, somehow.

Brimming. That's what it is. I want to get to a place where my sentences enact brimming. What's it called . . . a meniscus? Where you pour the water right up to the top, and it kind of hovers there? Frost has that beautiful image about somebody pouring water into a vase, right up to the top ("Birches"). And it just trembles there. It's that perfect fullness.

Jansen: An ideal?

Lee: Brimming . . . that's why I really believe it, too, when Rilke says you're only allowed to lament if you can praise at a very high level. If you can enact a very high order of praise, then you can lament. Because the fact that we're breathing has to be enough. That was what Rilke was saying. He was real tough about that. But I think in the last few years American poetry has come out of a poetry of complaint, not praising, and it was initially maybe rich. And it can continue to be rich if we remember that we shouldn't write out of complaint. We should write out of grief, but not grievance. Grief is rich, ecstatic. But grievance is not—it's a complaint, it's whining.

Jansen: Who has that grief for you?

Lee: Meister Eckhart. I'm kind of stuck there. I keep reading around him, reading the sermons. His ideas about the universe mind are interesting, but more than that his sermons are interesting as human acts. His sermons made it possible to speak straight from the universe mind. He wasn't addressing the congregation any more.

Jansen: Like Emerson again? We have your father, then Meister Eckhart?

Lee: I like different kinds of oral occasions. I'd like to use them all in my work. I wish I had a limerick, a riddle, a letter, a dream, a sermon.

Jansen: You have an interrogation in *The City.*

Lee: Right. I would like to have a telephone call. I would like all occasions of human utterance. *The Winged Seed* was my chance to throw everything in.

Jansen: Well, the section with you and your father is very much like a prose nocturne or fugue, a long prose poem, and then, there are more realistic—for lack of a better word—narrative sections. It seems as if you're trying to achieve some kind of balance . . . the brimming . . . finding the spot that doesn't spill over?

Lee: And I want to find a big form that somehow floats it all, and at the same time it has to take into account the tiny, the small. It's like writing the ocean . . . not writing about it, but *writing* it. How do you do that? Virginia Woolf tried that in *The Waves*, where each sentence was thinking. That's what it comes down to, that's what we're interested in. Consciousness. Where is it? What is it? Is poetic consciousness the mother of consciousnesses? That's what poets believe, that it's the whole consciousness speaking. The body, the mind.

Jansen: Yes, we're both pretty good judges of that. It's why we were created. Or what we touch when we put pen to paper. It's important for me that writing has to be tactile. Those are important things, the tools you pick up.

Lee: Well, when you think of it, for me, line even has to do with my elbow, right? Because, in a way, it's a kind of a dance of thinking.

Thinking, you don't just do it in your head, and your hand copies it. That's the way I experience it, anyway. When I'm writing poems, my mind is doing one thing, my hand is doing another thing that's in concert with my mind, but it's not doing what my mind is doing. Your whole body is writing.

Jansen: I think people don't always give enough thought to how embodied writing and reading is. Again . . . brimming.

Lee: Maybe the body is a condition of brimming? When you think about the fact that three billion cells are born a minute. We're literally brimming.

Jansen: You call the body "a bloody custard" in *The Winged Seed.*

Lee: "Custard" was wrong, right? It's more like "fountaining." Because I didn't know enough, then. I didn't know it wasn't a custard. I was only looking for the way it seems physically to me, the body. I didn't see its more basic nature . . . that it doesn't set. Three billion cells a minute. Reamy, three billion cells a minute! In seven years, we've got a whole new body. So we're literally brimming. And its significance has only begun to dawn on me.

   In the Chinese language, when we say, *qian*, "ten," that's the day before yesterday. The word, *qian*, means "in front of, or before." So yesterday lies in front of us. When you say *hotian*, that is the day after tomorrow; *ho* means behind us. So the future is behind us. To the Chinese mind, the future is behind us, the past is in front of us. We are backing up, blind, into the future. Which is true. Now, to the Western mind, the future is all before, so you leave the past behind. I think that's backward, because what you're looking at is in front of your eyes, is actually, literally, the past. All of this . . . the tape . . . everything . . . is going into the past, as we speak. Three billion cells a minute, as we speak, at that rate. So all of this is going away, and we're just falling into the dark.

Jansen: Like a star.

Lee: Right, it's already gone. So even when we look up at the sky at night, we're looking at a picture of the past. So when we look down and look around us, we're looking at a picture of the more immediate past, but it's the past. So we're constantly staring at the past. If we see this past and we turn on the news, and we get all this stuff and we think, Where's all this stuff coming from? It's precipitating here. And what do we have to change if we want to change the precipitation? Because everything is precipitation, everything is dew. It's appearing and it's going away. It's like foam, sea foam. If we don't like what we're seeing in the world, how do we change it? We have to change the mind that's producing it, right? Because the precipitate comes from the mind.

Jansen: Act better in the world?

Lee: Act better in the world.

Jansen: You have a poem in *The City in Which I Love You* called "Here I Am." It seems that the last stanza, ending with the line, "Here I am!," is your metaphysic. We've been talking a lot about what poems do. Maybe that's what your poems do? One person says, "Here I am," and then the reader says?

Lee: Yes, the reader feels it, too, right? So the poem is enacting this calling home of consciousness, and the reader gets it, too. So the poem is a kind of yoga. I always thought poems perform a service, like a church service. And I mean it in both senses. A long time ago, I tried to write a poem where every line was a part of the service. By the end of the poem, the service had been done. It was a yogic service—you'd been purified. You'd been anointed. Your original identity had been given back to you. You'd remembered you were a child of the universe.

Jansen: But again there's that sense of your trying to put poetic form around varieties of utterance.

Lee: Right. I understand what William Stafford said: the church service is a poem. There can be better poems and worse poems. Right now the problem with the church is that there's no poetry, and there's no mystery. It's all dogma and law. And without mystery there's no poetry; without poetry there's no religion. Religion now is fossilized poetry.

Jansen: There's too much meaning?

Lee: Too much logic. Did you ever see the mouth where lava is being born? There's a place in Hawaii where it comes right out into the ocean. It's this hot, red thing coming out as the ocean is cooling. I'm looking at that and thinking, Well, that lava thing, that's art. When the lava hardens into these patterns, that's religion. They're worshiping patterns that were once living. When you look at it, it's a record of something that was living. Art, for me, is the practice of that living—the mouth itself, what's really coming out.

Jansen: Again, passionate utterance. Your father gave you a lot of that, I think.

Lee: Right. And I think that Christ, that's a form of poetry. And if we don't read somebody like Christ and realize the upper end, the extreme possibility of poetry, then we're limiting ourselves. Or, if we don't read, for instance, anybody . . . any other poet who extends an extreme. There are all the extremes of utterance I would like to do, to hear, to say. It just seems really rich to me. But to speak from the universe mind, that seems the richest experience. Because then language becomes language in its spring, in its abundance . . . and what it can do, and what it can say. And then you have Neruda, you have Lorca.

Who else do we have? A lot of poets, right? Frost was doing that, right? Eliot? I have a lot of respect for poets who are in their nineties, writing, you know, brimming. I mean that's pretty exacting. Kunitz, say. Maybe changing is brimming? We just need to stay with the changes. But what are we steering by?

Jansen: And you?

Lee: You know, it's real easy for me. And that's why maybe I do feel bewildered by the work, by its body. It's sometimes there, and I'm all right. I can write four lines, and it's suddenly not there, and it'll come back, and maybe it won't. And maybe it will stay for fifty lines, and I don't know what it is. But its course is of the body, of another body, and you're writing it down, and it's a body of words. But then your vision moves away. So the work is bewildering.

Jansen: Is there a push-pull, a tension, you have with the lyric? There are more lyrics in *Rose* than there are in *The City in Which I Love You*. They're longer, but I don't want to say they're not lyric.

Lee: It's both. I value the lyric; I love it. I just haven't been able to do it lately because I'm just obsessed with this other form. Part of me suspects that my real poetry will come from my not writing poetry consciously, but when I'm doing something else. You have to do a lot of waiting. The waiting is even a pregnant part of it.

Jansen: Waiting is so much a part of your poetry, too. In "My Father, in Heaven, Is Reading Out Loud," your father is waiting, and it strikes me almost like a secret he has.

Lee: That he got his information the same way I did, like waiting under a lintel. (Lee reads the last stanza of the poem, "He waited merely, as always someone/waits, far, near, here, hereafter, to find out: / is it praise or lament hidden in the next moment?") I like *that sentence.* I wish I could have written it a bit better, but I can hear it.

I love sentences. I just love them. I think they're actually the backbone of poetry. A sentence is a unit of identity; it's not just a unit of syntax. It's partly a unit of syntax; in one of its reincarnations it was a unit of syntax. It *is* identity; syntax is identity.

A line, too, is an instance of identity. A poem is an instance of identity. It all has to do with presence, because a poem is a transference of potency. That's what art is. You've taken your heartbeat, your psychology, your brain, and you're transferring all of that energy into a medium, language . . . paint, chisel, and hammer. And you're transferring it into a thing.

Jansen: And there's waiting in that, too.

Lee: The waiting has to do with authority, hearing something that sounds like authority. And what does authority sound like? What does authenticity sound like? We should know. Because if we don't know the authentic, then we don't know the difference, even, between something like The Beatles and The Monkees.

If we don't know authenticity, we're going to get a lot of The Monkees. The practice of art is to recognize the authentic. Therefore everybody should be doing art? We'd be healthier. It's like that thing they asked Berryman's wife: did she think he would have killed himself if he didn't write poetry? And she said, I think he would have killed himself earlier. Poetry was what saved him. We always want to blame it on the poetry.

But why would I read, for instance, William Faulkner and hear the authentic? I was born in Indonesia. I'm a Chinese guy. How come, when I read him, it sounds authentic to me? What is it that I'm hearing? Passion. I don't even hear the story. I just hear the passion.

Jansen: Maybe it's also Faulkner's awareness of a dying system, like your father's awareness of a dying system in China?

Lee: He read that as the death of consciousness, right? Because in *The Sound and the Fury* what he was seeing was a new consciousness. That's what made him a genius. He took on what he saw, took it into his own art. He didn't write just one more straight narrative about the death of the antebellum South. He enacted the breakdown.

Jansen: And he does so much of that in the sentence?

Lee: Right, right. Again, the sentence. The sentence must be a unit of consciousness. When you're reading it, you're inhabiting that unit of consciousness. And in "The Bear" and in *As I Lay Dying* Faulkner practices the sentence like a kind of breath. You feel like it's coming out of his mouth, and the longer it gets, the more speculative it gets. It starts to say contradictory things, the longer his sentences get.

So he was trying to inhabit longer and longer frequencies, like trough and wave. Because if the sentence is a unit of vibration, let's say, he was trying to inhabit these longer and longer ones. Which meant that the consciousness he was trying to get to was a bigger one. Because the waves on that ocean are very long, so it's very vast.

Jansen: I think of that vastness, though, in Williams, too.

Lee: Yes, the speculation is going on in the line; they're so tight that every three words he's interrogating himself, he's speculating. So the whole thing is on sand, right?

I love thinking about poetry. I can think about it all day long. And I keep wondering, what is writing, is there writing? Is it just transcribing voice? Is there something else going on? Is there an independence going on to the writing itself? Because it's silent, right? It's possible, if we're writing, we can get to a new point, a new silence, a silence never heard before. When I read Rilke, I was beginning to hear silences I hadn't heard before, like in *Sonnets to Orpheus*: the silence after the gong, that was so large in Rilke. The only other poet

I was getting that from was Neruda. And before that what Christ said. And the Chinese T'ang dynasty poets. They'll say a few things, but the effect is actually a silence and a solitude. It's like their paintings . . . one little guy's fishing and the rest of the painting is all space. The silence is shapely.

So, I'm wondering, is it a poet's job to figure out deeper and deeper silences? Roethke heard a lot of pretty deep silences. It's even dangerous to talk about. But that's one of the effects of contradictions, "I wake to sleep and take my waking slow" [Roethke, "The Waking," *The Lost Son and Other Poems*]. But it's a contradiction, since the effect is a silence, and it doesn't sum up. There's no such thing as silence in the material world, and it's purely our intuition of God that makes us think that there is.

Jansen: Well, there's no such thing as a vacuum, so how can there be such a thing as silence?

Lee: And yet we know silence and solitude are two impossible states that exist. We're never alone. And maybe they're the first two intuitions that give us God-hunger. We express that God-hunger in different ways. Even Nietzsche, that's what he was dying of. Even as he spoke about the death of God, he was God-hungry. Hunger is an emptiness. That's why art is necessary. To remind ourselves of our solitude and our silences: that's our original state. That's what it comes down to again, then, that art is the practice of our original identity. And our original identity is that universe mind, right?

Jansen: Well, you certainly think strong thoughts about this.

Lee: I just love thinking about it. I fear sometimes that I think too much and don't act enough. And, I think, what action is best? It's the poem. What if one were to do that? To live life as though one were making art?

Jansen: That's what Rilke did. Or he seemed to come the closest to this ideal.

Lee: That would mean we would bring to every situation our whole attention? But that would be good; that wouldn't be bad, right? But who said art was supposed to save people? Maybe that's the wrong assumption? See how untenable all of this is?

Do you know that story in The New Testament? Where Jesus goes to a woman's house, and she brings out this jar of alabaster. I love this story. Jesus is going to die in a few days. When she comes out and she serves him this meal, she brings out a little vial of alabaster filled with nard. Nard, I guess, is crushed seeds. It's made into a medicinal balm, and it smells real good. She anoints his head and feet. And then she throws the jar onto the floor and breaks it. And Christ's disciples go crazy. They say that she should have sold it and fed a lot of poor people. And he says, "Well, she's preparing my body for dying; she's sanctifying it." And he says, "The poor will always be with you." And I thought, Well, he says a "smart" thing. And then he says a kind of personal thing.

The act itself, though, continues to be unexplained. And the reason is the act was such an excess that even the disciples only saw its practical value. Its value doesn't lie in its practicality. It lies in its excess. She breaks the alabaster jar because she can't repeat this act. So it only has one direction, the act. She can't go back. It's done. The resolution, the conviction, it's all spoken there. And, on top of that, she's taken this very expensive thing, and she has not done a practical thing with it. She has given it to her own divinity; she didn't give it to the world. And, of course, the other beautiful thing is that Jesus, his own body is going to be broken like the jar. What's best in him is going to be spilled. So there's that story within a story. What's interesting to me is to the extent that her act was an act of abundance, too-much-ness, brimming, ecstasy, outside, not explainable, unaccountable, unpredict-able, spontaneous . . . art, poetry. Praise. Praise is the state of excess, ecstacy. We counted up all the deaths; we counted up all the dying; we counted up all the terrible things in life, and guess what? There's still van Gogh painting sunflowers, there's still morning glories. There's an excess in the universe, a much-ness, a too-much-ness.

Jansen: Weeds still break open the cracks.

Lee: It's all this, things breaking out, things too much, things getting out of hand. That's somehow the thing itself.

Jansen: This was brimming.

Lee: I hope so.

Working to Hear the Hum

Laura Ann Dearing and Michael Graber

The following conversation took place in November 1996 under the auspices of the University of Memphis River City Writer's Series and appeared in 1998 in Crab Orchard Review. *Reprinted by permission.*

Interviewer: Some critics link your work to the visionary line of American poetry by Whitman, Hart Crane, et al. Are you comfortable being assigned to this vein? Do you strive for visionary moments in your work? If so, could you describe one of these moments?

Lee: As I was musing over the questions I found that, while they were great, they come out of an assumption that I don't necessarily have. If I can explain some of my assumptions, about writing and about our being here, then maybe some of this will come clear.

In the West I know that we are accustomed to thinking of the future as lying ahead of us and the past as behind us. We leave the past behind as we walk forward into the future. And because I think we're homo erectus, we see the horizon line. We have metaphors of life occurring to us at the rate of walking. We think we're walking toward a horizon into the future.

In the East it's very different, and I think this is an essential difference that might inform some of the subsequent questions. In the East our word for the day before yesterday is *chin tien*: it lies ahead of us. The day after tomorrow is *ho tien*. *Ho* literally means behind you. To a Chinese mind, the future is behind us, and the past is before us. To a Westerner you walk forward into the future, and you leave the past behind. To an Easterner we walk backward into the future and everything we see here is in the past.

Now, if we think about that, it's not only a difference in orientation, it's a difference in what we assume about reality. When we go out at night and look up at the stars, some of those stars have been dead for millions of years. So when I come out and look at them I'm looking at some late report. I am literally looking at a picture of the past when I look up at the night sky. Now to a Chinese mind this is a picture of the past, constantly. As we walk backward into the future, which lies dark because it's behind me, I don't have eyes in the back of my head. All of this is the past. The light coming from the ceiling, my voice, my coming into the room, the sips of water I took, it's all going into the past. We constantly live inside the immediate past. Where is the present? That is one assumption I want to make. And it seems something I live with day-in and day-out.

The second assumption I'm making is that this body itself is already the past. This body itself is the late report of an earlier body. Everything that occurred here, everything occurring here, is the late report of an earlier event. Our being here, telephone calls, plane arrangements, whatever occurred already to make this possible. So we are constantly living in the late report of antecedent events. That's my assumption.

As a result, I always assume that poetry is the voice of an earlier body. It is not the voice of this body. So that the voice we're hearing in poetry, being the voice of an earlier body, is the voice of a truer body. Because this body is not our true body, this body, the same way we look up at the stars and some of those stars are no longer there, but we see it, this body is like that dying star. We see it, but it is actually no longer here at a rate of about three billion cells a minute. As we speak, three billion cells a minute are dying in this body. We don't always know that, but if we choose not to know that it would be like somebody choosing to think the sun goes around the earth—when we know the earth goes around the sun. So if we know the body dies at about three billion cells a minute, it occurs to us at about the rate of falling.

Now can we realize that prime reality? That, number one, all of this is going away, fading away, this minute, as we speak. It is going irrevocably into the past as we see it. And we are falling backward into the future. When we go out we don't know whether we're going to find a five-dollar bill on the sidewalk, whether we're going to be hit by a car. The future is dark. All we see is the past. This is a long answer to the question about the visionary.

All art to me is yogic practice. That is, yoga in the sense that it means "link," or "yoke." What are we yoking ourselves to? Our true nature. Our original nature. And our original nature is an actual body, that this body is only a late report of. So for me to believe in this body is to believe in a shadow, a dream. I can only believe in the voice that comes from an earlier body. And that body happens to be much larger than this one. It's much larger, darker, because it's beyond seeing. We get glimpses of that body sometimes in dreams. When the light of mind falls on that body we see the feeder of that body, but here's a body beyond the dream body, which is even greater than the dream body.

So that's my assumption. That's always been my assumption. I don't understand the visionary, I suppose. I'm not all that familiar with the visionary lineage of the West. I've read Eckhart, and I've read some Kierkegaard, Hart Crane, Whitman. But it seems to me that the fundamental assumptions are different.

Interviewer: At an address at Eastern Kentucky State, you said, "The ambition of a poet is to write to a state of nobody-hood, to write from an anonymous source, and to the extinction of the personality." Yet you write very autobiographical poems—using yourself, your wife, your children as main characters. Please explain this dichotomy of using the self as subject matter, as a means of obtaining selflessness.

Lee: The subject of my poems is the voice in the poem. It's not the figures that adorn the voice. The voice is silent to these mortal, earthly, time-bound ears. It's silent, so what do you do? You sheathe it.

If you hear a conversation going on in the next room and you don't hear the words you can tell by the way the voice moves whether it's a mother speaking to a child, whether it's a mother reprimanding the child, whether it's a mother reading a story to the child, whether it's the mother telling the child a joke, whether it's lovers arguing. You don't have to hear the words. You can hear the rhythms, the harmonies, the disharmonies, in the voices and sentences. Those voices, those sentences, those frequencies, those vibrations, those naked voices, are more interesting to me than the words. The words are like birds that perch on this frequency of sound. And the voice is what I'm really interested in here. It's almost as if what I'm saying is the ostensible subject is the father, the mother, whatever is in that poem, but the deeper subject is the voice. Has this poet heard the voice? Because you can have a poem where there is no voice, but there are a lot of words. There is no voice from that earlier body.

Interviewer: How does that fit in with selflessness?

Lee: I always assumed we have no self. We go through, day-to-day, sub-personalities. I'm a father now, when I walk out of the house to visit my mother I'm a son, then when I'm speaking to you I'm a poet. Those are all sub-personalities. They are not eternal. There is a self, but it's earlier than this, and it's earlier than the sub-personalities that I walk through on a day-to-day basis, but the selflessness that I'm talking about is somehow extinguished and the nobody-hood is this larger body. Because it does not recognize any specific role—this larger body simply is, it's pure voice, and that's probably why I think that poetry is the instrument of that body more than any other art, because that body is pure voice, which you can't see. But you recognize it with your ear.

Our true body is a body made up of pure vibration, and we know this; physics tells us this is all vibration. You break down the plastic of this chair and it's made of molecules, made up of atoms. Atoms are 99.999% space. There is no materiality. This chair is 99.99% space. It is vibrating space. This is vibration. My voice is vibration. This chair is a coarse form of vibration; my voice is a higher form of vibration. Silent thought is vibration. The larger body has as much or as little materiality as this (chair). The larger body is truer than this, because it doesn't fade like this. The chair looks like it's going to be here forever, but it won't. These walls won't be here forever. These words already are gone. The selflessness, the nobody-hood, is not speaking these tinny versions of personhood, but speaking from an actual personhood. We've been duped, in a way, to think our body is our personhood, our job is our personhood. The whole universe is humming, is vibrating. It's that hum that I want to hear. That's the subject of my poems. But I can't write a hum. I tried that in one poem called, "From Blossoms," the last line says:

From blossom
to impossible blossom
to sweet impossible blossom

I thought that I just didn't want to say any words. I just want to make some sounds. The words are both a fortunate and unfortunate happenstance. We're lucky to have them so we can hear the underthing. We don't listen for the underthing. Our art is very much in danger. It's going to be just words. And we forget what we're trying to hear is the hum. Humming supports the chair; humming supports mountains; humming supports this body. To be a poet is to reveal the hum, which is "logos." It's pure mantra, that's what it is. Logos, mantra, Tao, law, whatever you want to call it. It's all one thing, it's the humming through the trees, through the chairs, through our bodies, the water we drink, it's all humming. If we're quiet enough we can hear it. And poetry is that frequency.

Interviewer: What is your take on the poetic aspects of narration, specifically, what are the factors that make a narrative poem a poem rather than a story?

Lee: Not everything we write on that page has the same vibrations. If we write an anecdote, the vibrations don't go out as far. If we write a story it might go deeper. What I listen for in narrative is such a wide hum that it encompasses all of our story. There's only one story. Every story we tell is telling that one story. I don't know what that one story is. One will never know it. We only hear parts of this great story. When I'm trying to write a narrative it isn't the specific narrative I'm interested in. Even though there's a strange magic that happens. The more specific you get, the closer to the hum you get. Faulkner gets it a lot. Sometimes I'm reading him and I don't even hear the words. I just hear the hum, for instance, in "The Bear" or in *As I Lay Dying,* when the dead woman talks. I hear that.

Interviewer: Is the hum different for the poet than it is for the reader?

Lee: I would think it would have to be. It would depend on what you're listening with. If you're listening only with these dying ears, that's what you hear. But if you listen with an earlier self, that's what you hear in poetry, or you hear its absence.

Interviewer: Is it the process that's important? You have to work to hear that hum.

Lee: Yes, absolutely.

Interviewer: It's a different work for a reader than it is for a poet or a writer, I think. There are two different realities. Would you say they are variations on the same hum?

Lee: Yes. It's varied in terms of its orientation. When I'm writing, I don't even know what I'm doing, because it isn't even writing. It's more akin to hearing. The writing is almost in the way. I wish I could *not* write. Just hear purely. And I happen to believe that if I were only hearing purely, that is work done in the first body. I think if I'd never published it, I'd still have done the work. And that's what Li-po was doing when he was writing his poems and sending them down the river. He realized, I've written these poems, the work has already been done, because he also believed there is only one mind.

Interviewer: Do you agree with the language poets' take on writing as a separate entity from the poet? That they try to write without involving the self?

Lee: When they say, "writing without a self," and I say, "writing without a self," it might be a little different. I write with a self. I don't believe in these sub-personalities. I believe in a true self. A self free of its temporal, earthly roles. That makes me nervous of the way the language poets talk about it. Sometimes some of the language poetry that is read is about writing, or literary activity. It's not hearing. I'm not really interested in literary activity like, Gee, I think I'll take an album cover from one of my children's rock-and-roll albums, like *Alice in Chains,* and cut it up, and mess it up on the floor, and say, Hey, there's a poem. That's literary activity. It isn't the hearing I'm trying to achieve. I'm not saying it's a lesser activity. I'm just saying it looks like literary activity. I'm trying *not* to write. The fact that I have to write is unfortunate. I'm just trying to hear something, so there's a difference. Occasionally, when I read Michael Palmer I think he's hearing something. Occasionally. And he's a beautiful writer. But in a way that's not available to me.

Interviewer: Many poets from a cultural minority have a lot of political emphasis in their poems, but your poems don't. How do you feel about politics in poetry?

Lee: We'll get as concrete as possible. I see something I don't like. Let's say that I see a man hitting another man. The minute I see it I realize what it is that I'm seeing. That is the late report of an earlier event in the mind. If I think I can break up that fight, and I've solved something, maybe, but I know that the problem I'm looking at is a problem of mind. The mind is the problem.

It seems to me that we are dealing with symptoms all the time. So let's say there's this body of humanity, and it's this pure perfect body. And we see lesions appear on it. And we keep cleaning up the lesions with none of us asking where are these lesions coming from. A lot of the way we deal with politics is like that. It would be like my son, when he was four years old and he saw something on television, or on videotape, of someone perpetrating some cruelty on someone else. And he'd say, "Come on, Baba, let's go save him." I told him, "This is already over, honey. If we get in the car and drive to L.A. there's nothing we can do." What are we going to do? This is the field of endeavor.

Our minds are the sources of all our pathology and neuroses. Prevention of that is what we should deal with. Art is one way to do that, unless we practice it as literary activity. Art, practiced as yoga, introduces only one body. If we look at the earth, we think, There's the earth and there's me. Well, the earth is teaching us differently. Whatever you put into the earth, you put into your body. Where is the other body? Whatever you put into the rivers, you drink. Whatever you do with that body, you do with your body. There's only one body; there's only one mind. Every time we see a precipitation of violence, rape, war, we've got a lot of work to do. If we don't clean things up, that stuff is going to keep precipitating out. Prevention on the earthly level, on the horizontal plane, is dealing with symptoms. It's not dealing with the source of our pathology.

The source of our pathology is mind. That is earlier than the body. So, we need to ask ourselves, How does the mind work? If I drive a car, and I'm teaching my son to drive, and I say to my son, "You keep your eye on that guard rail because I don't want you to hit it," what do you think would happen? He would hit the guard rail. We know when we're driving we go where we look. This is the way the mind works. That's why there is repeat behavior in abusive relationships. The child who was abused by his father abuses. He doesn't walk through life and say, "I will never do that." If we're looking at this we're recording it, recycling it. All we see are versions of the past. What we can look at, where we can drive to, to keep from hitting the guard rail. War, bang, disease, bang, we keep hitting the guard rail. And we keep saying, "Don't hit the guard rail, don't hit the guard rail." The Holocaust, bang, the Khmer Rouge, bang. We keep saying, "Don't do that," but we keep doing it.

The mind works by going toward what it sees. The artist is looking toward something else. Art is totally ideal. Otherwise it has no function. Then we are no longer legislators of the world. Poets are the legislators of the world, insofar as they deal with the first body. If you want to call it ideal, call it ideal. I would like to think of it as primary reality. We've mistaken this for primary reality. This is all over, this is finished. Art can get us to primary reality. And if we can't get there we're doomed to keep repeating what we see. Because that's the way the mind works.

Interviewer: What about the other arts?

Lee: Yes, the other arts, absolutely, like during van Gogh's time, when he was painting—throwing all that paint on the canvas, before everybody was painting on flat surfaces—and he was throwing paint on the canvas, people could literally not see the picture. In other words he had already turned his back on the past and really looked ahead into the future. But the picture that he saw, no one else could see. All of us are looking here. He was looking the other way. So nobody that walked into his brother's galleries could see those pictures. Now we can see it. Jackson Pollock, when he was doing his thing, we think it's paint thrown on a canvas. It is not. There is a picture. But he is seeing so far into the future, it's going to take us years to see that picture. It will take us years before we see a lot of those pictures. Rothko's pictures. It will take us years to understand the best poets we have. It will take us years to understand the significance of them. They've already relinquished the past. Fading away is the law of the universe. To align ourselves with that law is empowerment.

Interviewer: Words appear frequently in your work that most other working poets are afraid of using—love, beauty, and tenderness—for fear of being sentimental. Sentimentality seems to be the cardinal sin of poets today. Yet many of our daring poets straddle the fence of the sentimental, and the payoff is great. Discuss the great line of when a poem is emotional and personal, and when it becomes sentimental, perhaps in your own work.

Lee: I don't ever want to be sentimental in my work, but if there's a value to poetry, its value is praise. If I'm not praising I should shut up. Because I'm trying to line myself up with laws I perceive in the Universe. Yes, there is death, there is disease, but the flowers keep blooming, the ocean keeps coming home to the land, the sun keeps turning, so all of this is vibration. Let me go one step further: it's all song.

Now, that song is praise, because it just keeps making it up. Every spring it makes it up. Birds come back. Everything comes back. And to praise, that means spilling over, that is brimming. We master the bowl of this temporality by brimming it. We master it by staying inside it.

Interviewer: You have said before that you are a guest in the language, and that once we start speaking any language, somehow we bow to that language, and at the same time we bend that language to us. Do you think being a guest in the language has helped you or made it difficult?

Lee: I used to think that I was a guest in the language because I was Asian and I learned the language at the age of eight. But I see now that we're all guests in the language. And I think my being an immigrant heightened that realization. I'm sure that it has something to do with my wanting to write poems. Because it's a feeling of dislocation with the thing that you love.

Interviewer: In the poem "The Interrogation," the speaker says, "I'm through with memory." Does this explain the non-linear movement of *Winged Seed?*

Lee: Yes, my relationship to memory is very complex. I try to take my eyes off of it because my parents kept trying to turn my head and saying, "Look at this," and after years of this it dawned on me that I can't be looking at this because the more I look at it the more I repeat it. If a future is possible for my kids, I can't keep looking at this. But I can't help looking at it, because wherever you look it's the past. That's the strange thing about the eye. But I have to live with this notion or this intuition that all of this comes from an earlier realm. This body is the immediate past; I live constantly in the immediate past. So the past assaults me and every time it assaults me I try to purify it through art. I try to find the praise that's possible.

Interviewer: Frank Chin argues that the novelists Maxine Hong Kingston and Amy Tan do not legitimately represent Asian-American culture or an authentic Asian-American voice. Their success, according to Chin, is due to their insidious manipulation of racial stereotypes. Is there analogous debate for poetry? Is there an Asian-American poetry? If so, what are the formal characteristics? And finally, do you consider yourself an Asian-American poet?

Lee: I'll be honest with you, I've devoted about fifteen minutes of my life to that question. I like Maxine Hong Kingston's work. It meant a lot to me. I realize its importance on this horizontal plane. But if people find her work empowering that's the wrong way to go.

Interviewer: In the poem "My Father, in Heaven, Is Reading Out Loud," you said your father had you recite a book a month; I assume these are books of the Bible. You were his secretary, typing his sermons for him when you were old enough. You are more familiar with the Bible than most contemporary poets. How does this familiarity factor into your poetic ear? Do you find yourself working in biblical cadences or hymnal patterns?

Lee: I don't know the Bible all that well, but the logos is important. The idea, the reality of logos, is the law of the poem. The law begins from the first line. We're just there to unfold it. From the first line of the poem [Robert Frost's "Directive"], "Back out of all this now too much for us,/" [the end declaration] "Drink and be whole again beyond confusion," is already built into that line. A lot of it is walking that tightrope of the law. That's what logos is: it's law, it's Tao, it's iron, it's subtle. When we hear law in poetry we're not hearing human law; we're hearing universe law. In the poetry I'm interested in writing, and the poetry I'm interested in reading, which might be very narrow, we see a great painting, a revelation of law. Laws of composition, laws of color.

Frequently, an artist like van Gogh will see so far ahead of his time that it seems like lawlessness. Look at any archway. An arch is a great invention; it's not the rock it's built of, it's not the wood it's built of. It's a transparent law. How does it stand up? Law.

In the same way, sculpture helps us see space. The vaulted ceilings of gothic cathedrals help us see space. So, in a poem, it is not all about the words, the shaping of the words, jars spilling on the floors, a found poem. That's not interesting to me. Can we hear the law in the poem? That's the question.

Interviewer: You've been quoted as saying poetry is the language of longing; it tries to discover why we're all here at all. And also, for many years, you said, "I feel my years of homelessness and outward longing was because I didn't feel represented until the last few years when I realized my longing was for God." How do you feel this longing for God and other types of longing have affected your art? What role does longing play?

Lee: I never want to be away from that voice. Anything that distracts me from that law, that Tao, is a waste of my time. How many times have you turned on the TV and fifteen minutes go by and you realize, Wow, fifteen minutes have gone by and what have I been given? It's been taken from me—you've been drained, not fed? So much of the culture I feel drained by. But listening to poetry and looking at art, you feel fed because you're near the law.

Frost's great poems, Dickinson's great poems, Emerson's great essays—people read them and say they don't make sense, that they're lawless. No, he heard another law, a higher law. I don't give a shit about manmade laws; that's not what I'm talking about. I don't care about good and evil, modes of behavior. I'm talking about adhering to the same things the leaves adhere to, earth, the sun—something so elemental. The rest is chatter. An image is an idea, a true idea, an earlier idea than concept. Conceptual language feels like a later thing, and I want to get earlier and earlier and earlier. So images become more and more important to me. I would like to speak like cloud, moon, earth. Images are ideas. Concepts are late images.

Interviewer: How do you feel about the role of workshops as encouraging or discouraging different perspectives and voices in poetry? And what are your views on the creative process? Is writing mystical or is writing a learned skill?

Lee: I'm nervous about the word "mystical," because for me this chair is mystical, our being here is mystical. Is writing beyond temporal knowing? Yes, absolutely. Is writing a learned skill? Yes, certain kinds of writing, if you want to write a grocery list or the weather report. But not poetry. There are things you can do to orient the mind to make it available to poetry, make us more available to reading poetry and experiencing art. We're not always available to experiencing art. Just because we stand in front of a painting doesn't mean we're available to it.

Interviewer: In the past your subject matter dealt with family relationships. Are you still mining this seemingly inexhaustible source, or are you exploring different perspectives of the same relationships, or are you exploring different subjects altogether?

Lee: It feels to me that it's the same material, but it's at a different level. Because of the feelings that I have for my family, the feelings that have become big primary blocks, it's as if I'm going backward in time. Somehow I'm now a child. My feelings for my mother are like a big square block. I used to say, "OK, I have this feeling for my father, which is him standing in the tree, and I thought I saw him this morning," that kind of stuff. My feelings for my mother and father are bigger than me now. I can't tell about them anymore; they're like big shapes in my mind. My feeling for my child feels like a big shape. It has a definite body to it. That's the way it inhabits me. I'm stupider now than I used to be about my feelings, which is a good sign. I used to understand them. I thought I did.

Interviewer: You speak Chinese with your mother, but you don't write poems in Chinese nor read the old Chinese in its original text. Can you comment on a language learned but never committed to the page?

Lee: It haunts the way I am in the world. When I went to China I was amazed; first of all, we were there about eight hours and my kids were speaking Chinese, perfectly with their cousins. After a week, I was naturally speaking Chinese to my wife. She would ask me in English and I would answer in Chinese. And I was dreaming in Chinese. I would wake up, and my wife would be in the bathroom, and I would start talking to her in Chinese. It must influence the way I grasp the world.

In Hawaii, you have the island where the mouth comes out and lava is made. You see this hot lava pouring out and a few miles down the road you see the patterns and swirls that have hardened. That hardened stuff is culture. Worse, it's religion. Religion is fossilized art. Culture is fossilized poetry. I have no dialogue with culture. An artist ultimately cannot maintain a dialogue with culture. Art on the horizontal plane is not the full expression of that artist. Every great artist has to have a dialogue with something much more personal, urgent, and true than this dialogue with culture.

Interviewer: Your volcano reference seems very Blakean. What do you think of Blake's trying to systematize?

Lee: It is very dangerous. I find Blake a little too imaginative for me. This is my problem. When a haiku poet experiences what we call a haiku moment, that's not imagination. If he imagined it, it's not important to me. What he experienced was an actual moment of the eternal within the temporal, existing simultaneously, the earthly and the heavenly. I have to believe the haiku poet experienced something of the actual world. I know the poet weighs his words a lot. But I don't think that makes it less true. The imagination is the last thing we have to let go of. It's a scary place for me. It's a big mother. If we don't know the difference we will always be living in the inauthentic. We will always be duped. The purpose of art is to realize the authentic body, which is not this body. The East calls it Buddha mind; the West calls it Christ mind. That's too small. It's universe mind.

Interviewer: Did your father find some amusement in how your imagination worked all of that medieval technology and theology into a really hip take on the world?

Lee: I know he found me amusing. I know my mother finds me amusing. I talk to her and she puts her hand on my face and says, "Oh, poor child." I never read my poems to my father. He loved reading theology. And I used to love reading theology until I realized so much of it was elegant chatter. It's very seductive. It's not the practice of universe mind. I'm falling in love with the practice.

Interviewer: What role does revision play in your writing?

Lee: The poem comes out in an unsatisfactory version, because it was not equal to my experience. I take the whole poem, read it, put it into my mouth again, and let it stew there. My mind has its own digestive track. Then it will come out again in another version. And I don't know what will bring that version on. I might be walking down the street, and I'll pick up a leaf. The smell of that leaf might trigger that poem. And it comes out in this other version. Closer to something. When I envisioned writing memoir, *The Winged Seed*, I envisioned it as a long poem. Very stupidly, I thought, I am not going to revise a word. Because I had to see how really far I could go, whatever I said that minute I had to be nakedly honest to that impulse, so I did not revise a word. If anybody reads that book they'll see all kinds of problems, and my editor said we can get rid of these, but I said no, because I want to live with what I did. But now I feel a little differently. I wish I could stick the whole book in there and let it come out the other side revised.

All I was thinking was that I was going to blacken the page from the upper left-hand corner to the bottom right-hand corner. Literally, as if I had a black crayon I would just go like that. I said, "Now, go." And I wasn't allowed to think. A lot of those things were narrative, a lot were lyrical. I started thinking about the birds, and there it was. The self in *The Winged Seed* is the truest, most naked self I could manage. Now that's not valuable to anyone else except me. It's not worth two cents, two dead flies.

⋊⋌⋋⋌⋉

The More Poetry, the More Eternity

Patricia Kirkpatrick

The following conversation was originally published in the first issue of Water-Stone, Hamline University, *1998. Reprinted by permission.*

Kirkpatrick: Li-Young, you've said that in writing poetry, the poet turns all of his or her attention to an inner voice. And certainly in the poem you just read we heard many of the voices that we have come to know when we read your work. How do you turn yourself to that inner voice? Do you wait for it, do you pursue it, do you know when it's coming?

Lee: I guess all of the above. I do a lot of begging and sweating. That's a hard question—it's a good one. There's a long foreground to the poem. If you live your life in a certain way, it makes you more fit to receive the voice. I have to be paying a certain kind of attention, or a very special kind of inattention, for it to arrive, for me to hear it, because it comes from such a far place.

Kirkpatrick: How does a poem present itself to you? It sounds like you're not necessarily one of those get-up-at-five-o'clock-in-the-morning-every-day kind of writers. How does the poem get your attention?

Lee: I come to the desk every day and write, but sometimes I just sit there and stare at a blank page for two hours and nothing happens. It's about the soul for me. A lot of times you're walking along, and the soul visits you, and you put everything down, and you take notes or write a line, write the poem. Or sometimes you come to the desk, and you're rewarded for months and months of discipline and sitting there. I'm kind of superstitious. I feel like I have to be there. It's a little pact: if the soul doesn't visit me, it's not my fault—I was there.

Kirkpatrick: This is a related question. One of my favorite parts of *The Winged Seed* is when you talk about the native women in Indonesia telling you stories in which there were a lot of supernatural powers and spirits. How does superstition show itself in your life?

Lee: On the one hand, I'm very superstitious; on the other hand, I'm not. I do feel as if aesthetic consciousness is the highest form of human consciousness that we can achieve. That's the consciousness that art, religion, and the sciences came out of. So when we practice art—any kind of art, the writing of poetry or the making of paintings or music—we're practicing the closest thing to wholeness in consciousness. Although it is mysterious—what worked for one poem won't necessarily work for the next one, and you don't know what rituals will make it work—I try to ritualize it. But it's always a surprise to me. On the other hand, I know that it is a state of consciousness that can be achieved.

Kirkpatrick: Let me pursue this a little bit. You've talked about how the poet uses personal material as a doorway into more nonpersonal material. I'm quoting now: "We recognize poetic speech by its strangeness due to the presence of an unnamed speaker, a hidden subject. I recognize poetry by how 'other' it sounds." Could you talk about those qualities of otherness you like to capture in poetry? Are they technical things, or are they more along the lines of consciousness you were just talking about?

Lee: We know that not a lot of people read poetry because it's too dense. Poetry is dense because we, as people, are manifold in being. We have a physical body, an emotional body, a thought body, a soul, a spirit, and so on. At any moment in time we are all those things, so we are manifold in being. Often when we express ourselves—like when we buy bread—not all of ourselves is speaking. But poetic language is very dense because it is all of those levels speaking simultaneously, and it's manifold in reference. That's how I recognize poetic speech. It doesn't sound the way we're talking now. We're talking very linearly, and it's clear that one person is speaking to the other people. But it feels to me that when a poem is very successful, the center of it keeps shifting, and the audience isn't always clear.

Sometimes it's the stars you're talking to. Sometimes it's a woman or a man or a child; sometimes it's a man, woman, and child—it's all of those speaking simultaneously. That's what I'm a junkie for: that feeling, or that manifold quality of speech.

Kirkpatrick: Despite what you've just said, I know that you love plain speech in poetry, too. What are the dangers of following the path that you've just described? How do you avoid going overboard, or don't you worry about getting carried away with those voices?

Lee: I don't worry about it. I want to go overboard. What it's all about for me is passion. Desire and passion. The sun, moon, trees, rain—they're all made of passion. Passion holds the table up; it holds that flower together. The whole universe seems to me to be made of passion. That's part of the danger and beauty of being an artist: you're dealing with very ancient, elemental laws, material, and urges: the passion to speak, the passion to be quiet, the passion of inflection, the passion for innuendo. A sentence is a unit of passion. A line of a poem is a unit of passion. A poem is embodied passion. I like plain speech because I want the poems to be neighborly. It's like hearing from a passionate neighbor.

Kirkpatrick: In addition to those passionate neighbors, people associate your poetry with the sublime, with having qualities of high moral and spiritual purpose. I certainly feel that in your work and am deeply moved by it. But what do you do for fun? What do you do to work against the sublime?

Lee: Fun? Fun is sublime! Everything is sublime.

Kirkpatrick: Are there aspects of Chinese or American popular culture, for instance, that you're particularly attracted to? I'm thinking of you growing up in a household where a father spoke seven languages, and poetry was recited. That's not really the experience of most Americans; at least it wasn't where I grew up. So I'm wondering if there's any part of low culture that speaks to you as well as the high culture that you've been privileged to know in an intimate way.

Lee: I love low culture, the lower the better for me. And I love all kinds of bad culture.

Kirkpatrick: I don't mean it has to be bad!

Lee: I take in as much garbage as possible. Is that the question? Should I be specific about what bars I go to?

Kirkpatrick: Sure. And did your kids watch Disney movies? Do you listen to popular stations on the radio? Does any of that come into your consciousness?

Lee: It does come into my mind, not as an interesting subject to meditate on, to write poems about. It all just washes over.

Kirkpatrick: What part of your Chinese heritage takes place in your daily life?

Lee: I eat Chinese food every day. I eat with chopsticks. I've practiced a Taoist alchemy most of my life. I was involved in a small meditation and Taoist school. We went into the projects in Chicago and worked with gangs, and we went into senior citizen homes, and we worked with invalids. I love Bruce Lee movies. I used to go to New York Chinatown and see all the Hong Kong movies. And I have an older brother who doesn't speak any English—I use Chinese with him. But I'm losing a lot of it.

Kirkpatrick: Do you live in an extended family still? I know you did.

Lee: Yes, we live in an extended family. There are thirteen of us in a big building. We all eat together. And every morning the children go downstairs and say good morning to their grandmother, and on New Year's they have to do the three bows to the floor—the whole thing. And as they get older they get a little more and more shy about that, but we keep enforcing it and other little things, too. For example, if my mother is sitting on my left, I don't cross my legs so that the bottom of my feet faces her. You don't do that with your parents. I make my kids pay attention to that, but they don't get it. I tell them and they go, "Which way aren't I allowed to cross my leg?" "You just don't put the bottom of your foot facing toward your grandmother." It's that simple.

Kirkpatrick: There are certainly some images in your work that recur to become symbols. I'm thinking of the rose in your first book, or the cleaver that the Chinese butcher chops with at the end of *The City in Which I Love You.* How do images emerge for you and accrue meaning?

Lee: If an image comes to me, I don't write it down immediately. I do this little trick in my head: it floats up to the top of my brain, and I look at it with my inner eye, and then I let it go down again. Then it bathes in the back part of my brain, picking up more and more association. And the more association the image picks up, the better for me, because then when it comes out, it radiates everything that it talks about. It feels like I'm looking into a pond or a lake and I'm waiting for the image to come, and when it comes I sometimes snatch it too quickly. Part of my own discipline is to see if it goes back down or not. If it goes back down, let it go. But then if I haven't written something that I like in a week, it's hard to say, "Go back, I'll let you go." You have to keep letting it go back, and so it keeps bathing itself in all those associations and resonances.

Kirkpatrick: It sounds like your material is being worked internally a lot before it even comes to the page.

Lee: Each poem does its own thing, and demands different things of me. I'm a complete slave—that's what I feel like. I'm just a servant. When it speaks, I listen. When it doesn't speak, I'm bereft. I'm not the master at all. Some drafts are just a mess, like hundreds of pages, and some are one or two pages and I'm finished.

Kirkpatrick: I'm curious about your notion of the poetic line, and if the line comes into the work early on or later. And maybe this will be one of the questions that will start to make a transition from talking about poetry to prose.

Lee: I know this isn't going to inspire a lot of confidence, but I haven't a clue. If you learn carpentry, you do it and you get better. With poetry, I know less and less what I'm doing. But part of it is related to my own ideal to go toward unknowing. I want to write about what I don't know. The poem is basically the body of my thought/feeling, right there on the page. It's very different than speaking in complete sentences. Speaking in lines, there's more tenuousness and kinetic energy, there's more room for surprise.

Kirkpatrick: I'm wondering how you see the poet's role emerging at this time in America, given the particular point of view you bring to that question?

Lee: The poet's mission is to accomplish this whole mind and whole being in a poem. We have this poet in Chinese. His name is Li-po. He used to write his poems, read them to his washerwoman, then fold them up into little boats and send them down the river. He never showed them to anybody except this washerwoman. His poems feel very Taoist to me, and there's a belief among the Taoists that if you write a poem of whole mind, you don't have to show it to anybody. The poem is in the world already. Because a poem is a field of energy. And words are vibrations. And when we're dealing with words, we're dealing with very elemental things. When you make a sentence, you're putting vibrations next to vibrations. So when you write a poem, you have already manifested in the world this field of vibration. And it's a field of carefully negotiated harmonies and disharmonies and tensions and resolutions; it's in the world, whether or not it gets published or seen. You're bettering all the body of humanity. Because we are one and many. That's how I see the role of the poet: bring those vibrations, those fields of energy together and make them manifest.

Kirkpatrick: Thank you. Would you read a little prose [from *The Winged Seed*]?

Lee: This is about birds. I wish I were a big duck. I feel like a duck. I love ducks. I love to eat them, too. That would make me, I guess, a cannibal. I don't know what kind of bird I have in mind here. I used to go out with my father, and he would sketch figures of birds and I would watch, so this is about that. This is the place in the book where I've been going on at some length about my history, my ancestors. And then I end up asking, "But what do such stories have to do with me now?"

> My love—*this is basically a long love poem*—but what do such stories have to do with me now? My love, this is a story about dying. A story I tell myself, when, in a darkened room whose one window looks out to a brick wall, I can't sleep. This is not, however, a story about death. But dying. Dying is all. The earth filling to fill the sky with news of it. But only birds can reveal to us dying by flying. And so our eyes open to transparencies, hollow bones. The flight is nothing. The pattern. Aren't the turns and dives overhead shed as well as fled? Husk. Merely what's left behind by the dying. Isn't dying what

we're doing? For dying occurs exactly at the bird. Did I say bird? I meant word. This is a story about a word. One word. Dying occurs exactly at the word. Neither before, nor after. Neither in anticipation of its saying nor in the silence afterward. To read such dying as it occurs in the field of the air, to divine meaning is to stay with the body of the bird at every moment of its newness, every instant of the turn, the glance, the bird, its gestures. The word is itself and gathers into itself pure turn. Sheer glance. True bird opening in violence at the very brink of the dying bird who is nothing if not the assembly of glance, thrust, and turn. The way the bird fills the dying out. The way it is equal to the dying at every place. There, there and there. Cannot disappoint the flying. For it dies, and such dying is saying. Such saying must be possible so saying might achieve a here and now. There is no horizon in this saying. Only the dying without remainder. There is no horizontal groping from here to there, no allegorical grasping after that from this. And a word as it is saying is the very ground. Not the saying as the word as it was said. Only the word saying is both present and actual. When the bird is dying, the bird is not dead. The word dead is altogether another thing than the bird dying. And when the birds stand at rest, no flying is disclosed, though the sky remains filled with news of our passing.

Littleford: Thank you for reading that passage. To begin with, I should probably say that I wrote a paper about the use of the riddle in Li-Young Lee's memoir, *The Winged Seed,* and that's why I'm entrusted to talk about this with you. The passage that you were reading is that kind of very allegorical and poetic speech that is interspersed throughout the book. It takes up major parts of the memoir, along with the more narrative parts of your story. That is a new convention of the literary riddle: to combine poetry with prose, yet to write the poetry as if it were prose and in continuing sentences rather than with line breaks. I'd just like to hear you talk more about your choice of the riddle for *The Winged Seed.*

Lee: My own love comes out of this phrase in Chinese which means "big empty." In Taoist philosophy, there's this state that they call "don't know mind." It's the state of mind in which you don't know anything. They call it "the big empty." When you hear a haiku, the experience is "the big empty." Say something like, "Such a moon the thief stops in the night to sing." Wow, you know? You just feel a kind of spaciousness. Dickinson says it's like the top of your head being taken off. So you're not thinking anymore. You're just suddenly empty, but full. It was that kind of don't-know-ness that really interested me. There's the fascination, of course, and the satisfaction when you figure riddles out, but I like the state when you can't quite figure it out. Who is it—one of the poets, one of the old guys—said something like, "A poem has to escape the intelligence successfully." I take that to mean the same thing: a poem has to impart don't-know-mind. René Char said, "I leave you nothing to think." I think the poem isn't successful unless it imparts this don't-know-mind. That's why I love the riddle: it's so beyond you. It gives you that.

Littleford: The facts of your story are very dramatic, and you can see them as an epic, like Homer's *Odyssey* or a Hollywood movie, if you just presented the facts. Why did you choose not to write a movie?

Lee: I love the Old Testament and the New Testament. After I read those books, I felt the injunction that each of us is supposed to write a current testament, a gospel. The injunction isn't just to study the Old and New Testaments; you've got to write your own. When I read the New Testament and the Old Testament, too—it's broken down into two tendencies. One is a narrative tendency to reveal the presence of unaccountable forces. The other tendency I'd call "saying." Those are things Christ speaks. He says things like "The last should be first, the first should be last," and all of those things defy our intelligence. I don't think that's what they were meant to do. I think the figure of Christ is first and foremost a poet. What he was trying to impart by his parabolic speech was don't-know-mind. Big empty. I don't think we were meant to go in there and say, "Oh, this means I'm not supposed to eat fruit on Wednesday; I'm not supposed to wash my feet on Thursday." I wanted to write a book that had both the narrative and that saying quality. That sounds like arrogance now that I'm saying it, because who could speak that way? A lot of Buddha's sayings, too, are beyond comprehension. And the Upanishads. I wanted to write a sacred text.

Littleford: I love terrible things. With ferocity. There's something else about the telling of one of your father's stories. There's the story of your father's wonderful, miraculous escape while at sea in Indonesia, which is like Paul in the book of Acts, being miraculously saved from a shipwreck on the way to Italy. Anyway, you write that story, then you write about hearing that same story told by a friend of your father's, and you feel some sense of annoyance when the story is told. I have two parts to this question. First, is there a way that the drama of the family story could be overpowering? And second, is there a way that a meaning has to be pondered that makes it yours?

Lee: That's a great question, Laura. I had the feeling when I was little—and maybe we all do when we're very little—that our lives are mythic in significance. I think my father felt that, too. To this day, I've been trying to dismantle him and to see him as a man, but every time I try to do that, another thing comes up, and he's this mythic being again. Everything he went through is so mythic, it's so huge, it's perfect. His escape was miraculous: he almost died and came back to life. They had him in a suit, in a coffin—they were about to bury him—and he gasped and woke up, and he was like, What is this about? He gave his life over to serving the God he believed in and searching for that God at the same time. All of that stuff felt mythical to me when I was little, but I thought that was my secret. I thought, Well, I'm crazy, because everything feels big to me. Everything feels like it's here, and it's occurring somewhere else, too. I always held that as a kind of secret. I thought, Nobody would understand that. That's why when I started hearing poetry. I thought, That's talk that is double, small and large.

But that one place you're talking about, where I felt something like shame. I live in Chicago now, but before I lived there I was visiting my sister, and we went to a restaurant, and in talking to this waiter we discovered he knew my father; he attended my father's church in Hong Kong. My father was this evangelical minister, this big, big popular minister. He used to fill theaters like Billy Graham. He started telling us all this stuff about my father, and I felt ashamed. I thought that was my secret.

Littleford: That's a mystery to me, too, and has stayed with me. We'll just keep it in the riddle category. Throughout *The Winged Seed, A Remembrance,* your memoir, the word *remembrance* is important. In one way, the whole memoir is about memory and remembering. There is a ferocity, or intensity, where remembering is actually connected to creating the soul. There's almost a creational soul—if you don't remember, some of the soul is erased.

Lee: I do believe that. I hope this doesn't sound arrogant or mean or anything. I'm not sure if everybody has a soul. But I am sure that we have to work toward it. It's work to incubate a soul. I firmly believe there is a layer of memory that's personal memory. Behind that, there's something like race memory. I'm interested in getting through the personal memories to experience that bigger memory, that memory of the race. That's the job of an artist, to find personal significance but also the huge collective significance. And a lot of that is remembering—remembering what we are. That we're not just our personal history. We're not just who we are in this life span. We're something older. It's in ourselves, our bones.

Littleford: Another riddle! I'm interested also in *The Winged Seed* where you write about the physical act of writing Chinese characters. Can you talk about that process of forming those gorgeous ideographs versus writing phonetically in English?

Lee: When I was little, we used to take these sheets of paper, with grids, and we had to write a word a hundred times, over and over again. That's the way we learned to write. And my mother, when we came to this country, kept that up with us for a long time. We had these flash cards. She would flip the card up, and there'd be a picture, and we had to say the word. Sometimes she'd flash it the other way: it would be the character, and we'd have to say what it meant. When you're looking at Chinese characters, it's sad, because now they are very shorthand. They don't have all the strokes anymore. Like a seventeen-stroke character, now they've whittled it down to three or seven strokes. But I like the real packed characters. They are like little pictures.

For instance, my father's name had the word *country* in it. And one day I was writing the word *country* over and over again, and I realized, Oh, it's a spear enclosed in a heart. Suddenly I felt like that really explained him. He had a barb inside of him that wounded him and hurt him all the time. And that reminded me of my father. So it's like pictorial associations, not phonetic associations, though I'm sure that's there, too. But the picture-making mind is very important to poetic writing and making. Because the picture-making mind is an idea. An image is an idea in its most pristine form. And then you can break it down. If you say—this is a haiku—"I look into a dragonfly's eye and see the mountains over my shoulder," that's an image. It's full. It's also an idea. But if you say, "OK, the idea is, a large and a small and a small and a large" that's not interesting, you see? The image itself is the pristine idea. Some of my writer friends tell me, "Oh no, no, an idea is one thing, an image isn't an idea." No, an image is the first idea. An idea is like a denatured image. So those little pictures are ideas, you know? Like a country, or a spear: that's an idea. The picture of 'good' is a woman and a child. You know that's an idea.

Littleford: Also, the poems look really beautiful because the characters are so precise. It is wonderful. This will be my last question before we open it up. As a writer of both prose and poetry, can you speak about your experience in both genres: what are the challenges, differences, that kind of thing?

Lee: I know we have some prose writers in the audience. I hope I don't offend anybody, but I do feel that poetry is like a mother of all. I love prose, but I feel that what I want to hear is that manifold being speaking simultaneously, and one gets that in poetry. The best of Faulkner reads like poetry to me. I read *As I Lay Dying* like a long poem. The best of Melville reads like poetry to me. It's a chorus of intentions and everything being resolved in a sentence. There's that myriad, manifold thickness to it. When I wrote *The Winged Seed,* I went to New York to see my editor, and we were eating lunch and he said to me, "Li-Young, I think I know what you are doing." I thought, Oh, no, he found me out! and he said, "You're not going to get away with it. We didn't pay you to write a prose poem." And I said, "I'm sorry, but that's my ambition." I knew I wanted to write a long prose poem. The more poetry, the more eternity in it. That's the way I see it.

Rockcastle: "The more poetry, the more eternity"—I'm going to take that back to the novelist's desk and cry. As we promised, though, we are now going to turn the evening over to the audience for questions.

Question: How do you balance the demands of your everyday life with the demands of your art? Making a living, your family, doing your art—is there even a separation for you?

Lee: My first reaction is, I don't balance it—I'm always out of balance. One moment I feel like I'm not spending enough time with the family; the other moment I feel like I'm not spending enough time thinking about the poems. But the older I get, the more I realize that they have something to do with each other. If I allow it, when I'm cooking, aesthetic consciousness becomes part of it, and the meal is better. If I'm playing with my kids, if I get into aesthetic consciousness, the game is better. I really do believe in the yogic quality of art, so that it isn't something you do in that room, and when you come out you're a totally different person. It does go into the life, and the life goes into the studio; they feed each other. It's all yogic. That is, it all links us to our whole mind, our whole being.

Question: Do you meditate every day?

Lee: I do. But I don't think everybody has to do it. I think writing poetry is the highest form of meditation. I meditate every day in remembrance of what my father taught me. Otherwise, I'd be this raging maniac, I'm sure. But when I come upon those ancient Taoist manuals, when they describe what they call the highest state of mind a person can achieve, it's like they're describing what goes into making a poem. They say, "Oh, your mind becomes very precise but very open. It's very keen. The peripheral vision is very acute; even at the same time, you're centered." And I'm thinking, That's what I feel like when I'm writing a poem. Writing a poem must be the highest state; I've never felt anything like that meditating.

Question: In one of your reflections tonight, there were strong references to religious passion. You spoke about creating one's own testament as a very conscious reference to Biblical text. And you're probably aware that in many religious traditions there is a very vocal expressive quality alongside a very silent, passive quality. Poetry, of course, thrives on the oblique, and there has been a sense that poets have to use words, and they have to sound, they have to say things. But very often when they are at their very best, they're leading their readers and themselves toward a kind of silence that's beyond the noise of regular day-to-day speech. Do you practice any of these, this form of language toward silence, in your work?

Lee: I think I do. I love reading Eckhart. And when I read him I have the feeling that's what's going on. But I love that question because there's two kinds of silences: there's the silence when there's no noise, and there's the kind of pregnant silence. That's the one I'm looking for. That's when you know you're in the presence of sacredness. I do have the feeling that one writes toward it. It's that big empty again. When you read a great poem, it leaves you dumbfounded. You have nothing to say, nothing even to think. Your mind is just swept clean.

Question: I have a couple of questions about *The Winged Seed.* After your father died, you said your family burned its belongings. Did that really happen, and why?

Lee: It did happen, and I don't know why. When my father died, I remember I walked into the house. I said hello to my mother and walked into his room where he slept. My father slept like a rock, literally. And I lay down on his bed and fell asleep. When I woke up I heard a party or something going on. And all the relatives were there, and we were in the stage of hysteria. We were laughing constantly, for four days straight. We dragged huge garbage cans out into the yard under these apple trees, and we dumped everything in them and poured a bunch of gasoline in and just lit the whole thing up. And we stood under those trees for days watching the burning. With no bathing. Nothing. We took turns standing there, and our faces and bodies covered with soot. And part of the wood that we were burning, a huge splinter came flying out of the fire and shot right into my youngest brother's thigh. It went through his jeans and burned him. I don't know what that was about. But the whole time we were there drinking sour mash and laughing. We were hysterical. And we didn't know how to express it, so we just laughed constantly. It was almost crazy. There was no mourning, no crying. And when it was over, everybody kind of woke up and said, 'Wasn't that weird?' And we all went our separate ways.

Question: In *The Winged Seed* you mention that you kissed your father. Why?

Lee: You know, we weren't allowed to kiss him. I was real smart, though; I watched my father like the weather. So I knew there were moments I could sneak a kiss in, and it was OK. But other times you couldn't even get near his face. It was just part of the Chinese tradition, like not crossing your legs with the bottom of your foot facing one of your parents. If my father were sitting here in the middle, and if my brother were sitting on either side of him, we could not talk across him or behind him. Wherever he was, he divided the space. And we were never allowed to stand above his head, we were never allowed to touch his hat or anything having to do with his hat, and we were never allowed to kiss him. It was really special when he was really sick and I would wash his hair. I'd be washing his head and thinking, I'm touching his head!

Question: I'm curious about the dynamic of your family when in your book your father was cutting out pieces to make a paper temple.

Lee: We would help him cut things out, or he would draw little patterns and he would say, "You cut this one out." We were all involved. It was amazing to watch. My mother was there, and she would peel oranges for us while we were cutting.

Question: I wanted to know how your family reacted to your memoir. Were they receptive to it?

Lee: They didn't react at all.

Question: Did they read it? I assume they read it.

Lee: I don't know if they read it. I know my mother didn't; she doesn't read English. But I don't know if anyone else read it.

Question: When you were writing, did you come to a point when you thought, I can't write about this specific event for fear of dishonoring my family? Did that ever stop you from putting something in the memoir?

Lee: No. My feeling is, when you're writing about it, you're honoring it. I have a kind of law for my writing: I have to praise. If you can praise, then you can grieve. You're not allowed to just bitch and moan. You have to praise first. I end up praising even though I write some very unseemly, ignoble things about my father. The other thing is that I'm very shameless, almost wanton. I just don't care.

Question: Do you feel you have to have that attitude in order to be a writer?

Lee: Probably.

Question: How long did it take you to reach the point where you could have that attitude?

Lee: I was born with it. I'm shameless.

Question: Do you have a strong sense of self?

Lee: No. I've had people tell me before, "You have no sense of self, Li-Young." And I say, "Well, thank you." I'm not interested in my personal identity too much. I feel myself sometimes clinging to it. I get terrified because I'm getting older, I'm dying, or something like that. But I try not to cling to that. It doesn't interest me. Maybe my sense of having no identity has to do with my experience of being Asian in this country. Sometimes I look at the culture and I think, I don't see anything that resembles me. I guess it's a struggle with the personal identity that I experience. But there is a "nobody-hood." I like being nobody. It's like Emily Dickinson's thing: "I'm Nobody!" There's a richness to it. Of course, oftentimes, it's terrifying. You look around the culture and you think, I really am nobody.

Question: So you feel like you're defining yourself in a poem?

Lee: I feel as if I'm trying to unearth a self or discover a self. I don't feel like I'm actively defining.

Question: You lived in Indonesia as a child. Did you ever find Lami, the nanny you write about in your book, and whom you went back to Indonesia to find?

Lee: I went back to her village, but I couldn't find her. I went to the Red Cross. I had no address. I had a picture. The Red Cross woman looked at the picture and said, "Well, if you don't have an address, you're going to have to do this mystically." So I went to this mystic woman in a little shack, and she looked like she was eight thousand years old. Wow, I thought, the great mother, right? And she's smoking this huge cigar, and she has eight speakers behind her and a little receiver there with a tape deck. She takes the photo, looks at it, puts the photo down in the table, drips some wax around it and goes through the ceremony. And then she puts on the Rolling Stones. She cranks that thing up full-blast. I was going like this (puts hands over ears). My sister was with me. And the old woman is sitting in front of these eight speakers, smoking her stogie for about ten minutes. Then she turned the tape off and she said, "I can give you a couple of villages you might want to try, but I think you're going to be heartbroken on this trip." So she gave me a couple of villages and we went there. And I was heartbroken.

Question: I have a question about process. I've been thinking about the noting of vibrations, about words as vibrations. When you are writing poetry, do you speak the poems before you write them on the page, or is it an internal process, like an internal speaking?

Lee: It's both. Sometimes a phrase will come to me, and something will just tell me, "Don't write it down. Just let it rattle around in your head and pick up associations." And sometimes something will come to me, just a voice or something, and an edict inside me will say, "Write that down, see what it looks like." And I'll write it down. So it's all different; there's no one way to do it. You know what it's like? A poem is a lamp, and it's got just enough oil to last for you to write the poem down. And when that oil is gone, the lamp disappears, and you can't translate it to the next poem. There's just enough oil there to guide your way through that poem—that's it. The next one you start from scratch.

Rockcastle: And a novel is a big lamp.

Lee: It's a power station!

The Pregnant Silence That Opens

Indiana Review

The following conversation between Li-Young Lee and an audience at Indiana University took place early in 1999 and originally appeared in the Fall 1999 issue of Indiana Review. *Reprinted by permission of* Indiana Review.

>rrr~rrrx

Audience Member: How do you feel that your work has been influenced by cultural expectations?

Lee: From the very beginning my own dialogue has never been with the culture. In fact, that's a problem for me. I don't feel that my being or my work is a dialogue. It feels like a monologue. Throughout history, if we look at sciences, arts, everything that humankind had done, there's only been one subject. Only one.

Sometimes that subject is hidden, and a secondary subject comes to the foreground. But the real subject is the self. If you look at the Hudson River Painters, you look at pictures of rivers. But all you have to do is touch the painting. There is no river there. You're not really getting the river. Or van Gogh's *Irises.* All you have to do is touch the painting. There are no irises there. What you're really getting is van Gogh's sense of proportion, his sense of line, depth, the medium, color, volume, perspective. What you're getting is van Gogh's presence. If you think about it, and it's pretty amazing, the irises are a picture of him more than anything else. Or Frida Kahlo. Or anybody. The real subject is the presence doing it. I know we say: "Oh, there's no self." That's suspicious to me. When is there not a self?

Scientists used to say that artists were crazy, that artists are too subjective, while scientists believed in an objective field of observation. But they're revising their position, telling us that there's no such thing as an objective field of observation. Everything was a projection. So if I look at atoms and say, "That's order," or "That's chaos," it says more about me. It doesn't say anything about the atoms. We don't know anything about the atoms. Even if there's an apple on the table and I say, "That's an apple for me to eat," the word *apple* names my relationship to the fruit. The apple isn't saying, "I'm an apple for you to eat."

We don't see by the light of what comes into our eyes. We see by the light of who we are. So who we are is the big mystery. Now if I can change that word from *self* to *presence*, I would say that the only subject there has ever been is the presence. Our presence, in all its manifold significance. When we look at the irises and paint them, when we look at the Hudson River and paint it, the presence is the subject. It has always been the subject. It's hard to grasp sometimes, so we need an object, like the river. So it seems to me if the subject is the self, then that becomes a monologue. And if it's a rich monologue, if it's a pregnant one, then I would hope there are other people interested. But you don't think really about that. You're just trying to make a work that has the most fate in it. It's a dialogue with the work. When you're writing a poem, you're dealing with so many things such as fate, chance, law, lawlessness, your personal will, and there's this other will going on. Frost called it "braving alien entanglements." That's what he said a poem was. It's a picture of the will braving alien entanglements. It isn't a dialogue with Buddhism or Christianity, necessarily.

AM: Do you feel like your culture and your heritage are part of *your* self?

Lee: Yes, in inescapable ways. But I would say that I'm trying to write from an anonymous place. Some place that transcends culture, that is deeper than culture. Deeper than who my parents told me I was or deeper than who the TV tells me I am. And it's a deeper place than Eliot says I am. Or Whitman. But it's like we're all on parallel paths.

Personally, I look at the culture and I don't see any valid, authentic depiction of personhood. I'm an Asian male, and I look at all the depictions of Asian males, and I don't identify with those at all. But then I look at males in general, depicted in culture, and I don't identify with those either. The problem with culture is trying to find an authentic depiction of our personhood. And there's very few. That's the popular culture. Then you go to art. And you get more authentic depictions. But even in the art, it's limited. Eliot's depiction of what personhood is is very limited to me, as great as he is. I'm just trying to uncover an authentic personhood. That's probably an impossible enterprise.

AM: Last night you said that you spent two years painting peaches and that you discovered, Wow, there's so much in there that I don't see up front. If a peach is so complicated, how complicated is it then to write about personhood?

Lee: Well, when you write about the peach, I think you're writing about personhood. Whatever I say about it says as much about me as the peach. The object is infinitely ungraspable, which is probably why I'm obsessed with the figure of the lover in my own work. It seems to me that the lover is infinitely escaping me. You could be making love to that person and the essence of that person is not graspable. It's that ungrasped thing. When I'm eating that peach—eating and making love are very similar to me—the escaping quality of the reality of eating that peach is what I'm trying to catch.

I spent years painting and the early thing you do is outline everything you paint. After a while, you don't outline any more, and things begin to blur into each other. Our delineations of things have to do with context. It gets a little shaky. We're used to thinking of the self as something I could draw—a classical version of the self standing like that [*poses chin on fist*]. That's not the self. The self is much more fluid, bigger.

AM: How does the Buddhist goal of transcending or escaping the self fit in?

Lee: My small understanding of Buddhism is that they're trying to transcend the self as object. It was a great Zen Buddhist who said, "In all the ten thousand directions, it's the self looking back." You're never outside of who you are. Even if I said, "I'm going to write a poem in the voice of a rock," it may help you see things you wouldn't have seen, but it's you writing the poem. There's always this hidden person behind everything. And what I end up doing is projecting personhood out into the universe. I walk outside and it seems the whole world is speaking to me. The trees . . . mountains . . . rivers . . . creeks, rocks, clouds. I keep projecting personhood out there. There's no bottom to it. I can't get to a place where there's no more person here. I would like to.

It's treacherous and murderous sometimes to be a person. Art is a way to manifest complete presence. Let's take the word *self* away. Let's just talk about presence. That's better. I don't like the word *self* because it's so object-oriented.

Poetic language is so manifold. Prose means mostly in one direction. It's talking about that one thing. But poetry means so many things because it's an instance of total or manifold presence. Our psychology is manifold. We have consciousness, subconsciousness, all of that. It's not always accounted for in our daily life. But in art it accounts for all of who you are. Your fears, your sexuality, your body, your emotions—all of that comes into play when you're making a work of art. And for me a work of art is weak when it doesn't account for as much of who we are as possible.

AM: So what do you find to be the difference between painting and writing?

Lee: Well, there are obvious differences. In painting, the medium is so tactile; you're squeezing paint, you're mixing, there's the smell of the paint. While language has its own qualities. In my own painting, I just love making marks. For a long time, I had a friend and the two of us used to go on rooftops and do graffiti all over the place. I remember doing the graffiti and feeling that mark-making was a really primitive, primal thing. You see a wall and you want to make a mark. So we used to make marks with big brushes. We used to paint with tar. So right now when I'm working, I love mark-making. I love hand script. I love writing on the canvas. I don't do representation as much anymore. I spent years doing that. I love to make marks. I'm terrible. I see wet cement sidewalks, and I've got to write something in it. I'm the idiot who does that. Don't you love to make marks? I think that influences my writing too. I love writing in pencil on paper because I love to make marks on the page. Writing in a sketchbook is mark-making. I love the brush on the canvas. I love clay. The virgin piece of clay and you just fall on it. I love that.

AM: I wanted to ask you about your theory of prosody. Especially in *The City in Which I Love You,* the line lengths vary so much, from very long lines to very short lines.

Lee: To be honest with you, I have no idea about line lengths. I'm about as ignorant a poet as you will probably find. I have no theories of prosody. I know that when I'm working, it feels to me I want to find a line or a stanza that has the most fate. The most inevitability. It seems to me that you can say a thing that has been so fateful that it could not have been spoken any other way. Maybe it's arrogance on my part, but I don't want to reduce it to a theory of prosody. When we encounter our own work, we find the same principle that makes the leaves fall, that makes the earth go around the sun. There are fateful qualities in the language, and I'm trying to find those. So my line breaks, as long as they have a lot of fate in them . . . and they don't, always . . . fate and chance, they both come into play when you're writing a poem.

AM: I'm curious how and why the memoir came about and what you thought prose did that the poetry didn't.

Lee: Well, I don't know if it was prose. What I set out to do was write a long prose poem. It drove my editor nuts. I'll tell you how that came about. I was in New York one day at some function, and an agent came up to me and said, "You know, I think you could write some prose. Ever think about that?' And I said no. We kind of became friends, and we kept in touch, and one day I lost my job. So she would bring it up occasionally, and one day when she brought it up I said, "Look, I think I might want to do this." So I sent her a bunch of pages and she took all the prose poetry out of it and said, "I'm going to sell these fifteen pages." And I said, "Yeah, but they might get the wrong idea." And she said, "No, no, no."

So they got me a deal and that kept me afloat for a year. And when the editor saw the other stuff I was writing, poor guy, he went a little nuts. When the book was near completion, I gave it to him, and we had lunch, and he said, "I know what you're trying to do, Li-Young." And I said, "What's that?" "You're trying to write a prose poem. But you understand it isn't going to work. How are we going to sell a prose poem?" And I said, "Well, I didn't think about that." Because what I really wanted to do was to blacken a page with words.

With your hand script. Just start at the upper left-hand corner and blacken that page. Because I love to make marks. I could have just colored it in.

AM: It's a step up from the graffiti, right?

Lee: Yes, and I do feel that syntax is identity. The way you write a sentence says a lot about you and what you think the values of a sentence are. You write a sentence that's hollow and sloppy or you write a sentence that's just informative and there's no other dimension to it, that says a lot about who you are. So, for me, syntax is identity. I wanted to find out what syntax was. And the sentence was a unit for me.

AM: If your editor said that you could no longer write a prose poem, what did you do to make it an artistically satisfying experience?

Lee: I just kept eating my lunch when he said that. My dialogue isn't with him. It isn't with the marketplace. It's with something else. He said, "Before you get too deep here, let's publish this now." It kept getting more and more poetic. Little by little, the prose kept going away.

My feeling is that the closer something is to poetry, the closer it is to authentic complete being. I'm only interested in complete being. I'm not interested in anything else. I probably have ulterior motives in the subconscious, but I don't think I do. It seems to be an encounter to make a work an instance of manifold presence. I won't say "total" because that implies there's an end to the enterprise. It seems to me an infinite enterprise. A manifold presence.

Prose can't quite do it. Unless you're writing prose like Faulkner. Which is a little bit different. If you look at his sentences, especially in a book like *As I Lay Dying*, that's poetry. Much of *As I Lay Dying* reads like prose poetry. Much of *Moby-Dick* reads like prose poetry to me. And you recognize it by the manifold quality of the language. Suddenly the language begins to mean in so many different ways.

AM: You were talking about being as a kind of utterance. I was wondering if you had anything to say about silence in poetry. Is there anything you choose not to write about, either thematically or preferably, talking about words on the page?

Lee: I think I'm trying to use words to inflect the silence so that the silence becomes more palpable. I don't think silence is just a lack of sound. When I hear silence, there's a pregnancy in that word. There's a pregnant kind of silence, the kind of silence I want to inflect. It's like when sculptors use rock—stone—in order for us to experience space. You know the Gothic cathedrals? When you walk into them, it's space you experience. The verticality of space, but they achieve it by using rock. Otherwise, you can't point to it. It's transparent. Art uncovers space, silence. We're using words to make the silence palpable. Sitting there not talking isn't quite it. It's almost like you do that (bangs fist on table) to hear the silence afterwards. Wallace Stevens says, "I don't know what I love more, the beauty of inflection or innuendo." The sound of the blackbird calling or just after. So maybe it's the thing that happens just after you read the line of poems or the entire poem, there's a kind of pregnant silence that opens.

I remember reading Emily Dickinson. Sometimes I would read a line of hers and this big quiet would fill me. The Zenists call it a deep "a-ha." Wordlessness. The Judaic tradition says, "Be still and know that I am God." The blank page to me is both an illusion and a reality. Ultimately the voice has to embody what's on the page. And I know we can play around with the blank space on the page, but the proving ground is the voice. When you read it, if you can't feel the blanknesses of the voice on the page, then just scattering words doesn't do it.

AM: What role does vanity play in your work?

Lee: My body loves to pick up a brush, dip it in tar, and write on a wall. There's a physical thing. I don't think much about it. I realize it's vanity. And maybe that's the thing about graffiti I like. It's like the Tibetan sand paintings. They know that a wind can come and it's gone. And that's part of the beauty of the work. That you realize that something's going to come along and erase it. It makes it exciting and scary. It's like falling into an abyss.

AM: There seems to be a real strong sense of divinity in your work, and I'm wondering how the projection of the self relates to that kind of relationship?

Lee: The kind of poem I'm interested in is the kind that has manifold presences. Not just the personal self, but another presence. And if you want to say that's a divine presence, I'm comfortable with that. In a way, there's a kind of pregnant speech where you realize that there's a personal self talking. Yet there's the presence of a divine self. Art is the experience of the divine presence. No . . . art is the experience of an earthly profane presence in the context of a divine presence.

Now I know there's a lot of art where you don't experience a divine presence. That isn't interesting to me. That's actually a bankrupt enterprise. If you go too far down that road, that's a horizontal experience. It's like manifest destiny. Let's kill some more people. And you keep moving out. The self keeps moving out. I think the self has to move vertically, so that there's many presences speaking in a poem.

AM: Do you feel that writing requires a certain degree of vanity, an obsession with the self?

Lee: Yes, but that obsession can be really uninformed. If my obsession with the self has to deal with this personal, temporal self, that's dangerous. There's an eternal self and that inhabits a temporal self. If this obsession with the self doesn't lead us to understanding, it's just narcissism. Narcissism might be just a beginning. I know we live in a culture where someone called it "the heresy of self-love." We're not allowed to love ourselves. In a way, there's no other path. You've got to come back to the self. All the problems in the world are because we cannot master ourselves. That's the problem. All the social ills, all the cultural ills because of the misconception of the self. Artists are at the forefront of social change, not because they are actually involved in social things, but because they are actually changing and redefining what a self is.

AM: I would like to hear your thoughts about death in poetry.

Lee: I would say that death has to be in every poem. Because that's part of our manifold being. I guess in a way a work is contradictory. I remember my first painting teacher. We were all walking through a field together, and these geese flew over. He looked up and everybody looked up with him to watch the geese fly over. And they were honking. It was lovely. And he said, "The loveliness of that would be wasted on us if we weren't looking at it through our own death." Looking at it through your own death, suddenly the geese flying overhead is momentous, mythic. If you just look at it in terms of those are birds with four-foot wingspans, then it becomes nothing. Death is present in everything. But at the same time it has to have eternity. It's a perfect contradiction. Rilke said, "I'm looking for a contradiction to inhabit." Who would say such a thing? It's like saying, "Kill me." That's like when Moses says, "God, I want to see you." And God says, "Well, nobody sees me and lives." And Moses says, "Yeah, I want to see you." Who would want that? To inhabit a contradiction. Our death and our eternity. That is very hard. A salient work of art has to do that. We must never have an experience and think we're not dying.

AM: Do you feel poetry is essential?

Lee: It's mother's milk. We'd die without it. Nobody knows that, but it seems right to me. I think everybody's got it backwards except us because we practice some form of art.

AM: What do you expect from the artist that would make them produce mother's milk rather than Similac? What's the difference and where's the line?

Lee: Find the mother. At first we might like Similac. If you go to New York City, or L.A. or Santa Fe and look at paintings, 90 percent is Similac. I look through my poems all the time and think that 90 percent of that is Similac, and there's one little strand of real mother's milk. But find the mother, if we want to stick with that analogy. Contact with the mother. There's no other way to get mother's milk. In other words, no more second-hand stuff.

><del>~</del>~<del>~</del>

Riding a Horse That's a Little Too Wild for You

Tod Marshall

The following conversation took place in Memphis, Tennessee, in Fall 1996. It first appeared in the Winter 2000 issue of The Kenyon Review. *Reprinted by permission of Eastern Washington University Press from* Range of the Possible: Interviews by Tod Marshall *(2002).*

>-----~----<

Marshall: "The City in Which I Love You" is a very "twentieth-century" poem—a poem of fragmented memories, of exile, a poem that enacts a search for something to shore against one's ruin. On the other hand, the spiritual longing of the poem seems more of the seventeenth century, closer to the work of Traherne, Vaughan, and Donne. Do you think of your work as marrying these two poetic impulses? Or do you see the modern quest poem—*The Waste Land, The Cantos,* and others—as being propelled by a spiritual hunger?

Lee: I feel a great affinity toward quest poetry and certainly a lot of affinity with Eliot's quest, but I feel ultimately that there's an arc, a trajectory that's ancient as Homer. Every time someone asks, "Who am I?" that's the quest, and I'm sure it was asked by many, many people. There's something else, too. I think the impulse to write that kind of poem arises from the disparity that occurs when we realize who we are, but we think we can't live it. So for me, it's the realization of my identity and that identity as the universe. I am perfectly convinced that is what I am, the universe. I can't live it. Why? So the poetry comes out of that. The poetry comes out of a need to somehow—in language—connect with universe mind, and some-how when I read poetry—and maybe all poetry is quest, a poetry of longing—I feel I'm in the presence of universe mind; that is, a mind that accomplishes a 360-degree seeing; it is manifold in consciousness, so that a line of poetry says one thing, but it also says many other things. That manifold quality of intention and consciousness: that feels to me like universe. So that's why I read poetry, and that's why I write it, to hear that voice, which is the voice of the universe.

Marshall: For many twentieth-century poets, that voice only comes through in riffs, fragments, rather than a complete discourse— Eliot's ability to shape only a fractured answer to his quest. Pound's *Drafts*. Is this a fundamental change in poetry?

Lee: The way I read it that fractured quality is bad faith the poet experiences. Say, for instance, religion lets him down. So he turns his back on religion, and he faces the profane life. But there's a danger in that; in a way, it's a kind of death. A poet's dialogue is not with a human audience. Yes, the poem communicates: that's a by-product. When a poet writes the poem, the dialogue is actually with the universe, and if we don't realize that, our poetry and our art is in jeopardy. When the dialogue is carried on horizontally, with the culture, that is a lower form of art. When it is a dialogue with the universe, that is the highest realization of art.

Marshall: Would you say, then, that *The Waste Land* is a dialogue with culture . . .

Lee: Yes.

Marshall: . . . whereas, *Four Quartets* is a dialogue with the universe?

Lee: Absolutely. We hear big snatches of *Four Quartets* where it's a dialogue with the universe. I think he's most successful when that occurs; I think, though, that every artist goes through a period where our dialogue is with the culture. When we pick our clothes, it's a dialogue with the culture. We choose our spouse; sometimes, it's a dialogue with the culture. But ultimately, if we don't realize that our actions are a dialogue with the universe, then our actions don't have any power, capacity, because our horizontal dialogue is not as important.

Let's give the example of two people watering plants. If one person watering the plant realizes that what he's doing is a dialogue with his highest nature, the value of his watering the plant is very different from someone who's watering the plant and his mind is distracted. Two identical actions with different values; I am convinced of this. We can see that—well, look at the example of you bathing your child. If you're bathing your child and you're in a mind where you're totally present to what is going on in its temporal meaning and what is going on in its eternal meaning, the quality of your bathing your son is very different than if you're doing it distractedly. The value of those two actions are very different, just like when a poet writes poetry and realizes, when he's writing these poems, that he's having a dialogue with his highest nature, his true self, which is the universe, or he's just trying to write his poems in order to get into the *Paris Review.* The value of those two actions is very different, and the poem that comes out of them is different. So I would say that, yes, ultimately, all of us when we write poetry go through a period where our dialogue is with the canon—with Eliot, with Dante, with whom—but if a poet doesn't discover a dialogue that is more urgent than that, that is more personal, that is more anxiety-ridden than that, that has a greater tension and whose goal is a greater harmony: if we don't realize that, we're always going to be middle-shelf poets whose dialogue is with the canon.

Marshall: You have reacted very strongly against being pigeonholed as an "Asian-American" writer. One of the reasons such a title angered you was that you felt you are a poet competing with the other great poets—Keats, Milton, Donne, others. Do you think that that was your "culture phase" and you've gone beyond that?

Lee: Yes. It's a progression for me. The fine print of that question— "Where do you stand as an Asian-American writer?"—is a question about one's dialogue with cultural significance. I would say the answer is nil; I have no dialogue with cultural existence. Culture made that up—Asian-American, African-American, whatever. I have no interest in that. I had an interest in spiritual lineage connected to poetry—through Eliot, Donne, Lorca, Tu Fu, Neruda, David the Psalmist. But I've realized that there is still the culture. Somehow an artist has to discover a dialogue that is so essential to his being, to his self, that it is no longer cultural or canonical, but a dialogue with your truest self. Your most naked spirit.

Marshall: That makes me think of Keats who, in his earlier odes—particularly "Ode on a Grecian Urn"—wrote with incredible attention to the cultural, through allusions and such. Even in the poignant nightingale ode, one eye is on the canon. But this isn't so in "To Autumn" where he changes the dialogue from a concern about being one of "the great English Poets" to something larger and more poignant. He moves past his obsession.

Lee: Yes, and, of course, in order to be one of the great poets, you have to move past it. You have to discover a dialogue that is essential to you so that you can sing the songs, sing the poems, that only you can sing.

Marshall: What other poets would you point to as having achieved that progression?

Lee: I see it in Roethke. Many of Frost's great poems. The instances where knowledge is the way and he's speaking from a state of unknowing—or, I suppose, a state of knowing, because it is a state where you know in a manifold capacity.

Marshall: The poems where Frost is creating a "momentary stay against confusion"—but maybe not the one Frost thinks he's creating.

Lee: Exactly. In poems like "Directive" there are moments when I'm sure the poem escaped even him, and that's great, that's what I want, that kind of recklessness where the poem is even ahead of you. It's like riding a horse that's a little too wild for you, so there's this tension between what you can do and what the horse decides it's going to do.

Marshall: So do you return to Frost and Roethke and Eliot frequently?

Lee: And the Epistles.

Marshall: What about Williams?

Lee: I read a lot of Williams earlier, but lately I find that my assumptions differ from Williams's. I can't tell why this should be, but I assume the spirit, and the spirit is first. Even the body is spirit.

Marshall: And Williams is a very material poet.

Lee: Correct, and I can't see it because there's no ground. For me, apparent materiality has no materiality, especially now that physicists are proving that to us. The spirit for me—there's a lot of materiality there. I can't help but live with this constant feeling, this knowledge, that everything is fading away, there is no ground; there is no materiality to any of this, anything we see or touch. So where is ground? What is materiality? I can't assume the material world. It seems to me then that Williams's poetry is built on sand; it looks solid, but it isn't because it speaks from a self that is grounded in things. But things have no materiality; they never have for me. Things don't have materiality; every time I try to write about a piece of fruit or the body of my father, it disappears under my looking, under my gaze. It literally disappears. There's nothing there; it's all sound, all vibration. I've been looking for many, many years to find a ground, and I guess mind is the ground I've found. Mind is ground. So my and Williams's assumptions are different.

It seems to me that for Roethke there is an assumption even in his early poems, that spirit is ground. I felt that the voice is ground. The voice of his early poems is present in his later poems, too, except that it is more capacious—there's more for the voice—but it's there all along. That voice is ground for Roethke, whereas in Williams, he's almost pared it down to something where I don't know if he was listening for a voice. He was so concerned with apparent materiality.

Marshall: And is the poem on the page that is so important to Williams yet another dimension of materiality?

Lee: Yes, yes. I think it has to do with a backward notion of what the past and the present are. The Eastern notion is that the past lies ahead of us, before us, and the future is behind us. We are moving into the future. If we can see it, it is already gone. To get entangled with a phantom. At the quantum level of apparent reality, the most basic level, there is no materiality; it's sound, song. All of this materiality is the past. We are constantly inhabiting the immediate past. How do we get to a place where that's not going on? And I might add this: the fractured quality of a lot of twentieth-century writing comes about because frequently we've taken our eyes off our homeland, our true place, and we've looked at the past. The past looks fractured and confused; we forget when we're doing mimetic art; we think, Well, our art has to look like this reality, which is broken and confused and discontinuous. We've forgotten that this is not where we're supposed to be looking. We're not supposed to be looking forward, upward if you will, not back.

Marshall: How can one do this?

Lee: I suppose that through constant remembrance that all of this around us in this room is past; that all of this is fading away. It's an exercise of the mind to think constantly that this false identity is fading away and my true self or identity is fading away and my true self or identity is universe or God. There are certain assumptions that I secretly carry around, and I don't know if other poets share these. I assume that my nature is God. I assume that I am God, in my true nature. All of this, everything I see here, keeps me from remembering that. I would say that the way I try to do that is to live in constant remembrance of who I am. That I am not this. I am not this stuff that is fading away.

Marshall: But doesn't God also inhabit all this stuff that is fading away? Is there some differentiation, some hierarchy between the "hum," the song as manifest at the quantum level in this table, versus how it finds expression in you or me?

Lee: I think there is. First of all, it's mysterious but necessary for us to probe this assertion. When we say "All of this is God, too," we have to distinguish how God resides in all of this. God resides in all of this in law, which is transparent. So I would say, "Yes, all of this is part of God," because God is the transparent, subtle law that holds all of this up. That holds all of this together. But it's not this table. There is no this. All of this is an illusion.

Marshall: So logos as shaping force, whereas in human beings, logos finds embodiment?

Lee: In poetry, logos finds embodiment.

Marshall: Just poetry? What of other arts?

Lee: I don't know other arts that well. I look at them; my brother is a painter. But I don't want to claim that for other arts, because I don't practice them. Music, certainly. But everything that reveals for us, law, that's what logos is. Logos and law and Tao. They're the same thing. It's iron, absolute iron; autumn comes at a specific time and spring. It's iron. The earth goes around the sun. That's iron, but it's also soft, transparent. You can't point to it. So I would say that all art is yogic in that it yokes us to our highest nature; it reminds us of who we are. That's our true self.

The true self is the one that speaks, and it doesn't give a damn about the one that walks around in clothes. Sorry, it doesn't. That true self voice is the only thing that will last. The rest is chaff. But there is a deep, subtle law. We live in the midst of law all the time. You turn on a light switch, and the light comes on because it obeys certain laws. I talk to you from this distance and you can hear me; if I were to talk to you from a greater distance, you can't. That is governed by laws. We adhere to them whether we like it or not. Now, it seems to me that we can empower ourselves if we line up with it. And I don't mean by that going to church or not smoking pot or being Republican or whatever. I don't mean that. Those are human things. I'm saying line up with the voice that is the greatest inside you, that is deepest and smallest.

Marshall: In your vision, is it just that God or logos or law would allow cruelty? How do you account for cruelty?

Lee: I would say that human cruelty comes out of ignorance of who we are. If we realize that there is only one body and one mind—I don't mean realize it intellectually, but in a more fundamental way— cruelty is only possible when we are ignorant of who we are and who the other person is. It's God we're speaking of. Tod, there are not two minds here. This interview is one mind speaking to itself. Do you understand? This is one mind reminding itself, by question and answer and so on, of what it is, of who it is. This is what I believe. I don't experience this; there is a double experience for me. On one level, there are not two people talking here. There's one mind trying to figure this out.

Cruelty is when I mistake you for something other than God. Or I mistake myself for someone other than God. If I practice our mutual divinity, there is no way that I could be cruel. It's all practice. The logos is constantly enforced. All of this is fading away; that's part of the logos; that's part of the iron law. The words we spoke five minutes ago are irrevocably gone. Except as recorded here, but they will soon be gone from even this recording, even this text. That's part of the law. It seems to me that we must align ourselves with that logos, if we don't realize our true identity that we are the logos, we are the law, we are God. We have to practice mutual divinity.

Marshall: Sure, but there's that skeptical voice inside of me saying that Li-Young Lee and I can agree about this all day, but if we go out on Central Avenue in Memphis or Michigan Avenue in Chicago, there will be human beings bludgeoning one another, and there is not going to be a revolution in consciousness that will allow for the mutual appreciation of the godhead. And so we enact religious and governmental contracts in order somehow to mimic—maybe even parody—the law you're speaking of.

Lee: What I am saying is this. If we think of ourselves as separate countries I would have to say, "Well, I can't govern anybody else; I can't decide what anybody else should think." I only know what I feel and intuit. So the only thing that I can do is practice. I can practice mutual divinity. I can't ask anybody else to do it. It means, of course, the minute I wake up, I say, "Thank you." While I'm brushing my teeth, I'm saying, "Thank you." We have sixty thousand thoughts a day. How many times can I say "thank you" every day before my mind becomes blank, empty, nothing, and God can enter it?

Part of the practice of mantra, an Eastern practice, is the practice of emptying the mind, getting those sixty thousand thoughts so that they're not various thoughts, but all one thought. And when you can make it all one thought, there is no thought, there is something larger coming to inhabit you. So, in a way, I think of poetry as mantra work; you're trying to hit that one note and keep that note. "Back out all of this now too much for us, / Back in a time made simple by the loss": That's a mantra. "Time past and time present"— it's like a mantra. That's what it is to my understanding. So the only thing that I know I can do is practice it. I practice it. I'm not saying I've accomplished that; I'm saying I can begin again today. Ever since I was a child, that was a practice of living in constant remembrance of—call it whatever you want. Call it what the Sufis did; they picked the word for "fading away." So they're thinking it while they're drinking coffee, "fading away." "Fading away." They're looking out the window, and they're thinking "fading away." They get up and go to the bathroom—"fading away"—they look down at the table, and so on. That's all they're thinking. Some Buddhists think "thank you" constantly. It seems to me that all of that is yogic. It's exercise. It's making the mind.

Marshall: You have a rich ear, and it's reflected in your poetry. I wonder how those two things fit together: the desire to capture that "one note" that is the God, that is the universe humming, and the desire to write something like your line "the round jubilance of peaches" that is so full of luscious sounds. In earlier work, were you more concerned with creating an aesthetic texture than capturing this mantra quality?

Lee: No. I've always felt that aesthetic thinking was the highest form of moral thinking. It is the highest form of ethical and logical thought.

Marshall: The beautiful and the good as one?

Lee: Right. I still believe that. I think it's bad when poets say, "I don't believe in the beautiful anymore. Look at the world." Well, I say, "You're looking the wrong way. You're looking at the past. Poets should traffic in the ideal. You don't traffic only in the past." For me, as far back as I can remember, I was trying to hear a kind of hum, trying to feel it, and if I could hear or feel that hum, then the words just came and perched on that hum. If I don't hear the hum, then I have to make the poem out of words. But if I'm hearing the hum and I hear it very clearly, the perfect words like birds will come and perch on that line. They will be the perfect words. But if my hearing is off— if it's a little broken—and I'm faking it, then I'm putting words in there, making the illusion there is something underneath. No. I'm interested in the frequency under those words.

Is there that humming? And the humming, of course, is not only in the ear; it's your whole body. I don't write poems with my mind only. I know there are a lot of poems that when you read them you say, 'Well, this is a mentality writing,' and it may be a very great one. But it seems to me that poetry comes from my elbow, the ache in my knee. My hip. The soles of my feet. Literally. And whether or not they ache will determine what kind of language I'm using. The way my scalp feels. Whether or not I'm sexually aroused when I'm writing. I need to feel it with my whole being. You see, language for me isn't a mental thinking; it's like your whole body. Lawrence said that every man just writes with his penis, but you don't just write with your penis; you write with your whole being. Your fingers, your hair. That's what language is. It isn't some flaky dandruff; we keep thinking that "there's the world and there's language that's like some flaky dandruff that lands on it." If that's the way you think of it, then that's the way it is for you. But that's not the way that I experience language. Language feels to me like milk.

Marshall: Nectar.

Lee: Yes, like nectar.

Marshall: What of the formal impulses—you use couplets and other traditional forms, even poems that could be called sonnets?

Lee: The sonnet is a law, a shape of law. We think it's a literary form. No! It was first a law, and then it became a literary form. But there are certain laws: you can make this move, you can make that move, and you can make this turn in a sonnet. The *volta*, a turn. But some people treat it like it's an empty shelf, a shelf of books, and then you add the books and then you've got a sonnet. No. It's whether or not there is a turning in the sonnet, a turning of consciousness.

Marshall: The couplet, the sonnet, the villanelle as Platonic ideals, as aesthetic forms that have worked, that have successfully rendered the beautiful?

Lee: Exactly. And you know, when I did those poems, I wanted to use the word "accident," but the word "accident" doesn't have enough fatality to it. It was fatal that "Goodnight" was in couplets, and I have no explanation why it was coming in couplets, but I knew that the minute I tried to understand, the poem would stop, so I didn't try to understand. I let it come. Or, let's say I write a version of a poem and something's missing. I ask myself, "What's the law here that I don't see?" And then as I'm walking around one day or looking at the draft, I see "the couplet version," the actual poem, as though something in front of my eyes disappeared and I saw the law under it. And it was saying "couplets." So I put the poem in couplets and it works.

We deal in the invisible, not in the visible. That's what a poet does. It's not the visible world we're dealing with. And that's my argument with Williams, I guess—though I have to tell you that I love him. But he practiced poetry as though it's a secular art. It is not. It is the practice of the sacred. I would say that all religion is fossilized poetry. Poets are the real practitioners of the sacred. The priests, churches, they come after us. Let them build. They are already the fossilized versions of what poets come up with. That's the greatest calling for poets. Or we can write ditties. I see Eliot going wrong by putting himself in service to the Church. He should have realized he's prior to the Church. The Church is for him, the way King David said the Sabbath is for man. He put man ahead of the Sabbath. The Church is for us; we're not for the Church. When we make poems, that's what the Church is referring to—the voice that we hear when we write poems or the visions that artists see when they make paintings. Rilke called us "bees of the invisible," and he was right. It's not the visible world we're dealing with, because the law is transparent. You can't see a transparency, but we put words there so you can feel it.

There is a body prior to the words; words clothe that body. But it's not arbitrary; it's not "body" and then "words." If that body is humming, erect, it will magnetize certain words to it. You can't see radio waves; you can't see microwaves, but they're there. And there are these other waves: the great voice.

Marshall: What is the poet's responsibility toward the political? What do you understand "poetry of witness" to be? How does it connect to our culture?

Lee: I think that's complicated. I think it has to do with forgetting the poet's mission. I think we have a mission. When I first saw "poetry of witness," I said, "Wow! Now here's something right up my alley." And then I looked at it and thought, Oh, they're not witnessing the invisible. They're witnessing the visible. I wasn't interested in that. When I hear "poetry of witness," I think of the poets witnessing the invisible. The poet shows how the invisible is more real than the visible—that the visible is merely a late outcome of an invisible reality that rules us the way the subconscious rules us. Our dreamscape is larger and rules us more than this waking state. Beyond the dreamscape there is another consciousness that rules us. I thought it meant "poetry of witnessing the invisible," of witnessing our true nature—like Whitman was doing.

I think the poets of my generation have to make a break. We can't be poets witnessing the visible; we have to be poets witnessing the invisible. Or else there's no other hope. We know how the mind works. You keep witnessing the visible, then it will keep happening. In a strange way, a poet comes in cahoots with what it is he or she is putting down. They're saying, "This is terrible! Look at it! Look at it!" It would be like taking an abused child and replaying in his mind his father abusing him. Would that have a good effect or a bad effect? We know now that that repeated behavior in the mind makes it so he can't help but act it out. We've got to find a new recording for him; you've got to put something else in mind or he'll keep perpetuating it.

The poet becomes a perpetrator of those crimes when he or she reproduces those crimes in his or her work. I know that I have done the same thing, but that was out of ignorance or a fear that the invisible doesn't exist. In a way, Tod, I feel a kind of acceleration, a need to disillusion myself and stop thinking that the visible world is all that dear and that we can't lose it. That's a romanticism. We're losing it. From our body, three billion cells a minute are going! And it's faster than that three billion cells a minute rate; I just keep using the body as a point of reference. My words are disappearing faster than the cells in my body are reproducing, so all of this is going away. It's romantic, stupidly romantic, naïve ignorance. It's ignorance for us to think that we have to somehow witness all of this. No! That's not our business; the poet's business is to witness the spirit, the invisible, the law.

Marshall: What is the poet's relationship, then, with individual words? What sort of referential connection do you think they have to do with this vanishing world?

Lee: Language's mystery doesn't come from the notion that it doesn't refer to anything. What I find mysterious in language is that it's involved in a state of infinite referral. A flower isn't even a flower; it's a referent for something else. Each animal refers to something else. The whole universe keeps referring infinitely back. That's the way I experience it.

Marshall: An infinite regression of symbol?

Lee: Of referral. Every word refers infinitely for me. Certain words are more powerful. Because of my limitations—my personality—

certain words have higher vibrations than other words. Because words have vibrations to me, I don't experience sentences as a string of words. This is not a theory. I experience the length of a day, literally, as a sentence. One sentence. Or, I should say more clearly, as a unit of meaning.

Marshall: A measure?

Lee: A measure! I experience it as a measure. A sentence is a measure. But of what? It's a measure of information; it can carry information; it can carry time. You can write two sentences using different words, and they'll carry time differently. It can carry consciousness; it can carry different modes of consciousness. Certainly the way Neruda uses sentences is different from the way Frost uses sentences. There is more manifold consciousness in most Neruda sentences.

Marshall: You say a day is a measure—from rise to sleep. But there's overlap.

Lee: Right. Beautiful. So it's like sentence within sentence within sentence. A life is a day. In a way, during a day, from waking to sleeping, you get to enact your whole lifetime.

Marshall: The past overlaps into the future, then, in a continuum, and thus it's very difficult to pinpoint and capture the present, the essence, the eternal moment crystallized.

Lee: Yes, no one is going to capture it. Especially if they're talking about it. Because as long as you're talking about it, you're facing it. Sometimes you write three syntactical units called sentences, but the three of them actually create "a sentence." I heard somewhere that the word "sentence" used to mean "truth." If you said to someone, "You spoke sentence," then you meant that he or she said something that had authority.

Marshall: In many of your poems you use a short line; so a vision of the words stretching across the page is quite a departure from that. Can you talk about your lineation?

Lee: When I wrote those earlier poems, I was actually thinking in lines. So the hesitation you experience at the end of those lines, I experienced. That's the way I understood those lines.

Marshall: I feel those poems as moving vertically, down the page with a push. The movement in the memoir—we're pushed along in a similar way, but the pace is much slower.

Lee: Even now, in the poems I'm writing, although they have longer line breaks, I can see now that the sentence is my concern. I like the idea that the line breaks make notation for the mind actually thinking; I like that. But it's ultimately the sentence that I'm writing. Not the grammatical sentence, the measure.

Marshall: You mentioned earlier that—as you approach forty—the serious literary or cultural work that engaged you when you were younger is not important. And you also mentioned a desperate need for contemporary poets to reorient their work. What best captures the invisible? Do you ever feel that poetry, that language, isn't up to the task?

Lee: I'm writing more than I ever have. My experience is that everything is discourse; it's like a big roar, a big hum. Everything is language. Trees are language; birds are language. A bird is a cipher. A bird is a word. Beyond the word for bird, bird is a word. That's my experience. A tree is a word that refers to something else. The ocean is a word; each wave is a word. Now I need to figure out what I do with this richness. Well, of course, praise. It's the hardest thing to write, praise. What I've been writing, I hope, is just pure praise. I've been writing a lot, and I hope when I get a little time and go back to see what I've done that it's praise. The language of praise. I literally feel, Wow! Every leaf is a word. A vibration. A word is a vibration; a leaf is a vibration. Physicists have been telling us that: material reality is vibration.

Marshall: So you don't see yourself as ultimately despairing that you can't capture this litany.

Lee: No, no! I feel just the opposite. I feel grateful because there was a period I went through, thinking, It's all nothing, or something like that. But now, I don't know what's going on, I feel like it's all language. It's all conversing. Apples on the trees: I look at them and see all these words on the trees. It's all language. This table is a very bad form of language. This room is language; when you walk into this room, it's saying something. Your body reads it—whether you're comfortable or not. You're reading constantly. You walk into a restaurant: you know whether you're comfortable or not—by the lighting, the people, etc. You're reading. We're walking through the world reading. By the time of day we read, Oh, I should be home now. We're reading our children's moods, our wives' actions. We walk into a place like this, and think, Oh, I don't mind talking here, but I don't want to sleep here. Everything is language.

It isn't a big turning that I experienced, a reorientation from the visible to the invisible. It was a realization that that was what I was always doing, always hearing. I started to entertain some of the "stuff" that's in the canon; I forgot for a little bit that that was the horizontal, the cultural, and that wasn't the richest mode for me. If you look at the earliest poems in *Rose*, you'll see the vertical assumption. The assumption that the vertical reality was the primary reality and all of this was fading away, just "stuff" spinning off of that more important reality. The change was just in the realization.

Marshall: You haven't published much poetry for the last few years. Your first two books were quite celebrated, recipients of awards and such. How does the award and prize culture of the literary world affect one's work? Roethke, Yeats: you can point to numerous examples of poets who clip the articles and invest so much in reception.

Lee: I don't do that. I'm not patting myself on the back; I'm just saying that I find it boring. I don't clip reviews and articles and whatever. My wife did for a while, and then she stopped, too. She got bored, too. I think that dialogue is with the culture; I'm not interested in that. Look at it this way: it's like if you and I are having a serious conversation and someone over there keeps wanting to talk about *Laverne and Shirley.* We could engage that or we could just say, "No, I realize that this is what we're here to do." I see that horizontal dialogue with the canon, with the culture, as a waste of energy. I'm being very practical; it's a waste of energy.

Marshall: On the other hand, you rely, as someone who doesn't teach, on people celebrating your work and awarding grants and inviting you to give readings and such.

Lee: I'll tell you this. Let's say there's a man there and he's carving cork. Little pieces of cork. Someone comes up to him and says, "What are you doing?" "Carving cork." And not one pays attention to him.

And he does whatever he wants: he wants to do a grasshopper, he does a grasshopper; he wants to do a cup and saucer, he does a cup and saucer; he wants to do a toilet, he does a toilet. And then one day, someone comes along and says, "My God! Those are beautiful; I'll buy them all." It would be foolish of that man to change what he was doing. Why should he change his orientation? The dialogue for him was with his work, and he should continue that way. Why should he change?

Marshall: I see your point.

Lee: It's the same mistake as when we think our dialogue is only with the visible. Let's say the poet keeps telling himself, "I am a good poet, I am a good poet." And he works and works and works, and his book comes out and he wins the Pulitzer. Suddenly, the temptation is to put everything in front of one, to embrace the cultural dialogue, when the poet should be saying, "Get behind me; I knew I was good. You're late! Stay behind me! I'm still at the beginning here. I am the master of this dialogue."

Now that might mean everyone goes away or whatever, but I don't believe that that's important. I believe that when we line up with the law, the law wants to be revealed. It wills its own revelation; we're in service to poetry. Poetry is something greater than us. You see, the whole universe is a poem! It has no rational meaning. It has no reason for being. Yet it is. All of the laws, all of the universe's laws, are poetic laws. None of them are logical; all of them defy understanding. All of them are great. Everything we say about a great poem is true about the universe. A poem is a little universe. If we line ourselves up with that, the universe—God—can't help but support that. It supports itself. I don't mean to sound crazy, but I can't help but think that. Let's say I publish a third book of poems, and I think it's my greatest work. Nobody reads it. That's too bad. There may be a subpersonality inside of me that says, "Oh, gee, I'm sad." But the me that works and loves poetry will look at that and say, "Whatever. My dialogue is not with that. I'll have to be supported some other way. Go back and work at the warehouse. Whatever it is I have to do." Whatever my life, this huge momentous life of mine that is beyond me, whatever it offers me, that's what I'll do.

I don't like the idea that I depend on that culture. When a poet writes a poem, he or she has already created something better in the universe. By writing it! If he never publishes it, he's already created more value in the universe than someone else who didn't write it. That value comes back; it precipitates out into great things. Great things. I don't believe the writing of poems is unrewarded if you don't publish them. So it doesn't get rewarded *that* way, which is the most direct way we see. It gets rewarded other ways. Your health. The health of your children. Your mental health. The wholeness of you and your children.

There's nothing more heartbreaking than seeing a child suffer. And we think about the suffering that might be in store for them when we look at this culture. The highest thing we can do is practice art. There is only one mind, and so whatever we do in that mind— when we create more beauty there, more opening, more understanding, more light, when we shed more light in our own mind—affects the great mind. So you're creating value when you write a poem. And I mean material value! They've proven that on the physical scale, that when a butterfly flies across Tianenmen Square, it affects the weather in Florida. In minute and inevitable ways, everything is connected. In the invisible realm—which has more reality than the visible realm because the visible is dying and without materiality—when somebody writes a poem, when they open themselves up to universe mind and that universe mind is suddenly present in the visible world, the poet isn't the only one that gets the benefits. Universe mind comes down and that whole mind is a little more pure, a little more habitable. That's why we're the "unacknowledged legislators of the world." I never understood that until recently. We keep the world from falling apart, and they don't even know this! Not priests. Not ministers. Not rabbis. If we stop writing poems, you'll see this world go into such darkness. They won't even know what hit them.

Marshall: Quite an imperative . . .

Lee: Yes, and many poets are giving up that large mantle; they're saying, "We're witnesses of the visible." No. That's not our original mission. Our mission is witnessing the invisible and making it revealed in the visible so that everybody can line up and know what they're lining up with. Like Whitman—lining up with the cosmos that they are. They aren't lining up with the Pope or with "good behavior." The true self is beyond good and evil, and all poems are the voice of the true self. When you read a poem, you're hearing your true self. The more true self we uncover, the better for all of us. If you never publish another poem, but you write those poems, you're already doing work in the spirit world that is absolutely necessary.

Marshall: So what would you say to a pessimist who says, "OK, Li-Young, but what about all this tawdriness—*Baywatch*, Las Vegas, the O.J. trial—that commands such popular attention? Do you really think that this 'invisible' stuff affects that?" What if the skeptic just rejects the Platonic premise of your argument?

Lee: If all the poets in the world stopped publishing, we would still be doing vital work. If no one read poetry, we would still be the "unacknowledged legislators of the world." We are still at the gates winnowing the visible. Publication is secondary; we're doing it in the spirit realm already. Thoughts are like radio waves. They're finer than radio waves, higher in vibration; we don't have an instrument that detects them. Thoughts precipitate into action. If we don't like what we see, we're going to have to change our thinking. The mind is the only field of endeavor, the only field of work, that is fruitful to work in. It determines actions, which determine civilization, which determines health care reform, and on and on. But the mind is the first circle. If we work in the second circle, we don't know the outcome. The poet works in the first circle. All the time. The outcome of invisible things is always visible. But unfortunately, we always want to deal in the realm of the outcome. Visible things are always just a reporting in the visible world; as poets we want to deal with those things at the source. We should want to deal with the cause, not the symptom. The poet is the one saying the best and brightest things to a reader: "You're God; you're cosmos; you're universe." The poet is walking around saying, "We are the universe. You are the universe; I am the universe." That's what Whitman did; that's what King David did. What the hell are we doing? I see our mission as much larger than witnessing only the material world. And it isn't to report on a twenty-years war. Twenty years? What is that? The news is that we are the universe. That's the only news there ever was; that's the only news that the poet reports that lasts. We want to hear the news. We need to hear the news.

The Presence of an Eternal Mystery While Folding Clothes

Marie Jordan

The following conversation took place in 2001. It appeared in the Summer 2002 issue of AWP Chronicle. *Reprinted by permission.*

Jordan: You call your new collection of poems, *Book of My Nights,* a book of lullabies. Can you explain how these poems can be understood as lullabies?

Lee: I have the feeling that a line of poetry is the articulated dying breath. We sing a lullaby to a child because he doesn't want to go to sleep. Maybe the child is afraid of sleep. So we sing to the child to tell him it's OK to go to sleep. In the same way that a child doesn't want to go to sleep, I think sometimes we deny our death. We deny that it happens.

Jordan: So the child's sleep is a metaphor for death?

Lee: That's the way it feels to me. I was hoping that this book basically says that it's OK to die, and so the book is kind of singing us into our dying. I don't want to seem morbid, but it feels to me that the process of dying is actually dying into a greater presence. It isn't lessening, it's actually more. And we die into greater awe, greater splendor, greater terror, and greater presence.

Jordan: Did you have that theme in mind as you were writing these poems?

Lee: I think it became clear to me as I was writing them.

Jordan: When you speak of breath, how are breath and poems related?

Lee: Poems and breath are related in basically the same way that breath and utterance are related. That is, when we speak we use outgoing breath, the exhaled breath. The exhaled breath is the dying breath, while the inhaled breath is the in-feeding breath. So all human utterance is our dying breath articulated.

Jordan: And the inhale? Do we inhale the poem with our breath?

Lee: Well, let me back up and try to answer this way. Breathing is a wheel. It turns in and out, inhale, exhale. Now, I don't want to get too esoteric here, but I'll mention the fact that as we inhale, our bones and muscles actually get very compacted, harder. When we exhale, on the other hand, our bodies become very soft. Ancient Taoists, so I'm told, believed that upon inhalation, our ego-self becomes very inflated, while during exhalation our sense of ego and body diminishes and we become more open to a deeper, bigger presence. What I find of interest, though, is this: As we speak, what we mean gets disclosed in opposite ratio to the expelled breath. That is, as breath dies in exhalation while we speak, more and more of the meaning of what we're saying gets divulged. Frost calls this "the tribute of the current to the source." Was it Blake who called it "proceeding by contraries"? Meaning is born as the breath dies. In the case of poetry, the meaning that gets born is manifold, saying one thing but meaning many things. And in this way, a poem is a paradigm of human living. As we perish, the meaning of our lives is revealed.

Jordan: Theodore Roethke said he wanted poetry to extend consciousness as far as it can go. He said that he sought to write poems that try in their rhythms to catch the very movement of the mind itself. Do you think along the lines of Roethke, in terms of the mind?

Lee: I do. But let me say that I understand all poems to be projections. And to study those projections is to begin to understand the projector, the mind, or ground, of the projection. Let me add here that by the word *mind* I mean what the Chinese mean when they use the word *shin*. That is, mind *and* heart. A poem is an image of the maker, as a human being is an image of God. But a poem doesn't simply transpose being. It also proposes possibilities of being. A poem is also a proposition. It isn't just a naturalistic copy of the projector. Or maybe it is, and an integral aspect of human being is its tendency to speculate or propose certain ideal modes of being. Poems make very important propositions by their enactment of certain presences we may never envision if it weren't for the poems. Does this make sense?

Jordan: This seems especially true in *Book of My Nights*. In your two previous books, *Rose* and *The City in Which I Love You*, there seems to be an underlying wrestling with self and God. Now you seem to be far more intimate with the unknown, and with God. That wrestling, like Jacob's pulling at the thigh of God, is missing. Did you feel that when writing these poems?

Lee: I felt it in my life. I think that because when I was young I defied my parents, I projected or transferred all the god-presence onto my parents and the world around me. Part of my own evolution or development as a person is to try to recognize that presence is in my being, too. God's presence is in the cells of my body and deep in my subconscious. God's presence is not only out there in the world in trees and oceans and birds and people, but it's in me, I hope. In the new poems I was more successful at that. I was more open to what somebody called "the invasion from the inside."

Jordan: Your new poems appear at once semiotic and mimetic. They are fluid, diffused, and disseminated, yet you maintain an analysis of universal relationships. Do you see your poems as being beyond language, or metalanguage?

Lee: The thing that obsesses me is always beyond language. Language is almost an inconvenience. I have a feeling that no matter what kind of art we're practicing at some point we become hyper-aware of our medium. If we're painting it's paint and if it's writing it's the language. But if we don't at some point move beyond our hyper-consciousness of language, we're stuck in the land of the medium. On that plane, only the relationships of words to other words is available, while the relationships of words to their ground, mother-silence, on the one hand, and to the concepts they name, on the other hand, gets abandoned. That would be like seeing the significance of people only in relationship to other people, in other words, only as social units. Meanwhile, their relationship to the ground of their being and to their individuality is disregarded.

Jordan: You have said that we are all guests in language and once we start speaking our language we bow to that language and bend that language to us. What do you mean when you say that we bend language to us?

Lee: The beautiful Mexican poet Octavio Paz said something like, "The difference between prose and poetry is that in prose you use language and in poetry, you yield to language." It feels like there's this weird dialectic between us and the language. I can't tell whether we just yield to it or we bend it. Maybe both. Sometimes it feels like we're bending the language. Maybe it's a process of self-making. I can't tell.

Jordan: What, aside from language, does the poet have to work with?

Lee: It's not just language that we use to write poems. We use silence, too. In fact, I think we use language to inflect silence so we can hear it better. I suppose that's why I love Emily Dickinson. I love her the most when I don't have the feeling she's fooling around with language, but up against something she can hardly say. What we're actually seeing is the language straining to say something.

Jordan: What do you mean by inflecting silence?

Lee: Inflected silence could be explained by the way everything seems quieter after you hear a bell ring. It's almost as if we're using language, but the real subject is silence. The silence is primal. I hope that after a line or stanza there's a silence imparted to the reader.

Jordan: Are there different kinds of silences?

Lee: Yes, different colors and shades. The deepest possible silence is the silence of God. I feel a poem ultimately imparts silence. That way it's again disillusioning. It disillusions us of our own small presence in order to reveal the presence of this deeper silence—this pregnant, primal, ancient, contemporary, and immanent silence, which is God. I don't know another form of language where this is possible, except in poetry.

Jordan: I see a circular form in your new poems, going toward and coming back, and the life-death tension between poles. You take risks moving from deeper to more daring levels of consciousness, including the dream-state subconsciousness. There remains a tension between poles, a day-night, child-parent, and light-darkness. You call it "miles of the sea arriv[ing] at a seed."

Lee: It feels true when I'm writing the poems.

Jordan: What do you mean by the silence being God?

Lee: Do you know the verse in the Bible that reads, "Be still and know that I am God?" *That* kind of stillness, and silence. I think a really good poem can impart a stillness which is God—which is also awe. I would say that disillusionment is revelation, and revelation is apocalypse, and every poem is apocalyptic. On the one hand, we have ecliptic things that hide and on the other hand, we have apocalyptic things that reveal. The writing of poetry is writing that reveals, but doesn't just reveal a personal presence; it reveals a transpersonal presence and the dualities of that presence is silence, stillness, and the saturation of presence.

Jordan: Is the appearance of birds in *Book of My Nights* a metaphor for transcending or taking flight from the temporal?

Lee: No. I love birds.

Jordan: You mean they're just birds, nothing else?

Lee: They're birds and everything else birds can possibly mean to us. Ah, there's that thing again. To me everything in the world is saturated with luminosity and meaning so you could say that birds are just birds, but they're everything a bird could possibly be in billions of years of evolution. What does a bird mean to a billion-year-old man?

Jordan: Of the many recurrent images in this new collection, the most frequent is birds.

Lee: I did worry about repeating myself. Sometimes I felt I was writing the same poem over and over again.

Jordan: I'm reminded of something Galway Kinnell said: "If things and creatures who live on the earth don't possess mystery, then there isn't any."

Lee: That's true!

Jordan: To carry that thought further, Rilke wrote that touching mystery requires loving the creatures that surround us and becoming one with them so they can enter us.

Lee: Is there anything that is not saturated with meaning? Even when I write about my father or mother, they are very much my father and mother. At the same time they are more. They are whatever a father and mother could possibly mean to us.

Jordan: Another of the images I find arresting is folded clothes, folded and unfolded laundry compared to life and death, like the folding of nights and days in *The City in Which I Love You*. In *Book of My Nights* you write about lying down on folded and unfolded clothes— the life and the death.

Lee: If I look around, everything that goes on is saturated with meaning and mystery that I can't quite get my mind around. I see it and sometimes I can verbalize or find the verbal equivalent or correspondence in the world. Doing laundry is an instance. I do laundry every day, or watch my wife, kids, or my mother do it.

We're always doing laundry, and I come into the presence of an eternal mystery while folding clothes! I don't know why, but it feels that the world around me is saturated with another presence, mystery, and splendor, all the time. It's a matter of cocking our heads the right way and seeing it. Poetic presence is there all the time, even while doing the laundry.

Jordan: You've been likened to Theodore Roethke, Walt Whitman, and William Carlos Williams. Do you feel their voices echo through your own?

Lee: I read them with love so I suppose you can't help but have them influence you on some level. Isn't that why you read, too, Marie? You can't help but take them inside you.

Jordan: You've also been compared to Rilke, especially with your first book of poems, *Rose*. Was he an influence in those early poems?

Lee: That is a funny thing. I hadn't read Rilke yet when I wrote those poems in *Rose*.

Jordan: We're told that the first poets we read will always be with us and have an indelible influence upon us. Who were the first poets you read?

Lee: The poets my parents recited in Chinese. The Chinese poems they recited gave me the sense that they were instances of the small consciousness embedded in, or reading in, a larger consciousness. Particularly the T'ang and Sung Dynasty poems they recited. These poems have that echoing feeling of a voice speaking within the context of a larger voice.

Jordan: Were there other influences?

Lee: My father taught us English by reading the King James Bible to us. He was a Christian minister. The consciousness of the Bible stays with me, the questions that the kings asked of the prophets in the Old Testament, "Is there a word from the Lord?" When I come to the page to write a poem, what I'm doing is asking, "Is there a word from the Lord?" That is basically what a poem asks.

Jordan: Is this true of the poetry of the T'ang and Sung Dynasties?

Lee: There is a tradition in Chinese poetry that a poem is a model of psyche. Psyche is a model of cosmos, and so a poem is a model, or an instance of cosmos. It's a little instance of cosmic presence. The Chinese, especially the T'ang and the Sung Chinese poets, believe that the poem is an object through which to contemplate or experience cosmic presence. I happen to feel that's true.

Jordan: I understand also the classic Chinese poets' intimacy with nature and the belief in the past having accumulated much of civilization's wisdom is the authority to draw creativity and inspiration. How do you see your work in relation to nature?

Lee: Well, the human psyche is embedded in nature. Products of the psyche are finally projections of nature.

Jordan: I remember your saying you can't dance with your left brain. When you say that art must exercise the whole being, do you mean art in general?

Lee: The wonderful poet and teacher I studied with in Brockport, New York, Anthony Piccione, could never remind us enough times that poetry is the art form that engages both sides of the brain;

therefore, any time we read a poem or study a poem we're studying the human psyche. The ideal is the human psyche well-informed of all its parts; I mean, an intellect well-informed of the body, a body informed of the intellect, and both informed of the feeling faculty, and so on. When I write a poem, I want all of me present. Poetry is the one art form that explicitly opens channels to both hemispheres of our brain. My hope is that when I write a poem my body is present in the language as well as my mind, intellect, heart, and feelings. It's about that total consciousness and total presence.

Jordan: Do you think your life as a poet began when you were a child and you began transposing letters of words and spelling them backwards, as you tell us in *The Winged Seed?* When did you first take pen to hand and write your first poem?

Lee: That was when I first started to learn the English language. The words seemed *saturated.* Words like *yarn* or *bird* or *tree* felt to me saturated with meaning. That's when I really was taken with the English language.

Jordan: The painter Magritte was taken with resemblances of the real, and ridiculed representation as being the same as the word. I think of his *Betrayal of Images*, the painting of a pipe with the words at the bottom, *Ceci n'est pas une pipe.* This is not a pipe. The word and the image are not the same.

Lee: As far as I can tell, every word is a name for a concept. The word *the* names that concept we have of the-ness as opposed to, say, the word *a* or *an* or *any* or *every.* The word *tree* names our concept of a tree. Words refer to our concepts of things, not the things themselves. Cavafy said that a poet is a member of the city of ideas. He said it was a great honor to be a citizen of that city. I agree. And I sometimes think that while the word *tree* refers to our concept of a tree, a tree itself is one of God's living things. Or maybe the tree itself is God's living word concretized. The universe is a poem of God. But if words name, and a *tree* is a living word, a tree is a living name. A living tree is one of the names of God.

Jordan: Is there a connection here with the first chapter of the Gospel of John, "In the beginning was the Word and the Word was God"?

Lee: Absolutely. The Word is Lord. That idea feels very real to me. It's not a linguistic tool, but a mode of being. Being-in-the-Word, which is being-in-God. Being-in-God is our primordial, absolute condition, the condition of the psyche's embeddedness in nature and nature's embeddedness in God. Poetry is the language of that condition characterized by saturation of meaning, being, presence, and infinite potential.

Jordan: Let's talk about illusion and disillusion. You speak of art as a form of disillusion.

Lee: I have the sense that the world around us, the whole universe, in fact, is saturated with presence: terror, wonder, splendor, and death. Sometimes we do all we can to create illusions that it's not. Art comes along and disillusions us in order to uncover this original saturated condition. That's the great thing about art, and why many people don't read poetry. I don't know if they can stand that kind of saturation of meaning and presence because with it comes not only splendor, wonder, and awe, but terror, horror, and death. You can't get one without the other, and so we do everything we can to stay in the illusion.

Jordan: You have said that art directs us to uncover sacred reality. Do you mean art demands this of us?

Lee: Sacred reality is the saturation of presence in the world. Wind and trees and clouds and people and rocks and animals are all saturated with presence. The saturated condition is the sacred condition. There has always been only one subject—*being.*

Jordan: Your poems speak of your childhood, of fleeing China, and your family. Your 1995 family odyssey, *The Winged Seed,* centers on the life of your father, and as Ed Hirsch says on the jacket, it's a book of "intense . . . metaphysical questions . . . excavat[ing] and exorcis[ing] the past." You write about the secrets and mysteries you lived with for years. It was difficult and painful for your mother to discuss the events of the past and to reveal to you the truth about your lives. What does she think now of your writing your family story for others to read?

Lee: It's kind of complicated. She thinks I'm fooling around by writing poems, as if I should get a "real" job. But I think her attitude has something to do with the fact that she doesn't speak English. The

English-speaking world doesn't have much reality for her. If I say I'm writing our story in English and people who read English will read it, she doesn't seem to mind. I thought about this years ago because it was is if whatever we did in this country didn't quite count, that somehow we were not included anyway. Our vote or opinion didn't weigh as much so everything we said or did didn't matter because we weren't natives. I think she is unfazed because she thinks our story couldn't possibly interest anyone.

Jordan: Do you read your poems to her?

Lee: Once in a while I translate a poem for her. Her idea of what a poet is would be the classic Chinese poet like Lao Tzu or Li-po. She has such respect for them. When she gets together with her family they sit at a table and eat. One of them will start reciting some passage of Lao Tzu, Li-po, Wang Wêi, or the philosophers. When that person stops reciting in the middle of the poem, the person to the right completes the poem. They have a high regard for the writing of China. My mother can't believe that I'm as serious as any of those poets, so I don't weigh in at all comparatively. Every time I translate a poem of mine for her, I'm aware it's not Li-po, or Tu Fu or Su Tong Po. The poems fall short so I don't translate them very much. I'm an unenlightened poet if I'm a poet at all.

Jordan: In China the writing of poetry has never been thought of as a career, has it?

Lee: That's correct. My mother looks at me and says, "You're not enlightened." Those poets were enlightened.

Jordan: Do you write every day?

Lee: I have tried to put something on paper every day. It doesn't always work. My habits are erratic. I love working at the kitchen table. I have a study and sometimes I am organized. I have drafts of poems with a rock on each draft. I know what's going on at first, then within two weeks it's a mess. I am so undisciplined.

Jordan: Do you think that it's important to have discipline?

Lee: I don't know. I was raised disciplined in many ways. My meditation, for example. I thought writing was similar. There is an inner discipline to it, and I always have my ear listening. I'm always asking, "Is there a word from the Lord?" Whether I'm washing dishes or taking a walk, I'm always in that asking mode, so that's its own form of discipline. My whole life is writing. I'm doing it all the time.

Jordan: What decides the form of your poems?

Lee: It's my body. I read the poems with my belly and the soles of my feet, my hips, arms, and my neck. My body encounters the poem. If I read a line, I can almost feel my body say when the next line should happen. It's a very visceral experience for me. I don't know if it translates at all into the poem, but I wouldn't know how else to do it. I don't have any theories about form or line. I'm really unschooled. I'm ashamed to say it, but I am.

Jordan: Have you ever been part of a writing workshop?

Lee: Yes, I have. I spent a year at the University of Arizona, and I dropped out. I thought about studying literature at SUNY Brockport but also dropped out.

Jordan: Tell me about the experience you had in class reading *Wuthering Heights* aloud. That had a strong influence on you.

Lee: I had a wonderful teacher at SUNY Brockport. His name was Peter Marchant. There were about five of us students who met once a week in his office where we read *Wuthering Heights*. He made shepherd's pie for us. We ate the shepherd's pie and drank tea, and he would begin reading, then pass the book around, and each of us would read aloud. It was an incredible experience. It changed my world. I remember after reading the book, walking out of his office into the night air and feeling as if there were no threshold between my experience of the book and my experience of the world. The book was so present. Reading it aloud became something I took with me into the world. World was book, and book was world. When we finished, we started reading D. H. Lawrence out loud and the same thing happened.

Jordan: How important is reading aloud?

Lee: When we read, we read projected presences. Some of the problems with the state of reading in the country, and the world, might stem from people not being able to read presences, not knowing how to read the presence a poem projects. On top of that they may never recognize that it's a projection they're reading. And if they never recognize that they're reading a projection, they never learn to interrogate it. Is it a whole presence that's being projected onto my mind's screen? Is it dismembered presence? Is it hysteria that's being projected? Ignorance? Intelligence? Anger? Compassion? Love? What presence gets imparted by, say, a Dickinson poem? Or a Blake, or a Stern, or a Tsvetayeva?

Jordan: If we read with our whole presence, then reading another whole presence can become that icy fusion Dickinson may have been referring to when she said, "If I feel physically as if the top of my head were taken off, I know that is poetry"?

Lee: That's what Dickinson was talking about, if I understand her correctly. It does feel like the top of your head has been opened and you're somehow spacious. She follows that by saying her whole body goes cold, and I disagree with that.

Jordan: Do you think reading the unsayable within a work can be taught?

Lee: I have to believe it can be or I'd feel as if there was no hope in the world.

Jordan: I'd like to talk more about poems in your new book. You often use flower and fruit imagery: *Am I the flower, / wide awake inside the falling fruit?* from "Hurry Toward Beginning," and also the surprise of honey, occurring as the taste of itself within a line of a stanza: "Look again / and find yourself changed / and changing, now the bewildered honey fallen into your own hands, now the immaculate fruit born of hunger" ["Night Mirror"].

Lee: I wish I could insert a little piece of butterscotch in the book.

Jordan: Recurrent images such as rooms, wind, stars, moon, trees, books, clocks and the sea echo through *Book of My Nights*, each tolling with complexities and paradoxes through the prevailing lyric lullaby rhythms. Are those images part of an organized plan or an intended structure?

Lee: No. Just obsession. I almost want to apologize for it. I could have written about other things, but these are the things I was obsessed about at the time. Rooms and wind and stars and clocks and sea . . . so I didn't plan anything at all.

Jordan: And roses. Always the roses. You love roses, don't you?

Lee: I do. I bought roses for Donna, my wife, and they're on the counter now and dying. They're the most magnificent things, even when they're dying. They just get more and more beautiful. The edges are kind of rotting, and there is something so gorgeous about them.

Jordan: The image of the rose makes its appearance and moves through each of your books. For instance, it appears in *Book of My Nights* in the short Whitmanesque poem, "Heir to All," which speaks of endings and beginnings, of going into autumn knowing its name and inheriting the "unfurnished rooms inside the roses."

Lee: I think they're probably the only flower that is just as beautiful as they're dying.

Jordan: How much do you rewrite?

Lee: I do rewrite. But revision is a process for me of uncovering. I have the feeling that when I'm writing there is my will and then there is this bigger mysterious will, and the two of us are in some sort of negotiation on the page. A lot of times when I revise it's because my own will is too present in the first draft. I have to uncover the other, the deeper will. Sometimes the Big Mind doesn't make it the whole way to the page. It gets refracted or distorted.

Jordan: What was it like for you to go through the editing process of *Book of My Nights?*

Lee: I always have the feeling when I revise it's like unearthing. I'm uncovering. I was very lucky that my editor, Thom Ward, helped me in that process. He was a close reader. I had the feeling that he was trying to move me closer to that presence I want to achieve. Another wonderful reader for me was Anthony Piccione. If there was something wrong with a poem, it wasn't as much of a process of changing a line, moving a word or adding language—he wanted me to clarify the figure. It was almost archaeological. It's the kind of revision I've always done since studying with him. It's the kind of editing my editor, Thom, was moving me through as well.

Jordan: A dream editor.

Lee: He's wonderful.

Jordan: How often do you write a poem that fails? You've said at times that art is a glorious record of great failure.

Lee: I have claimed my poems to be failures when, in fact, what I should do while writing a poem, is to say thank you and move on. We should be grateful when a poem visits us.

><del>↔</del>↔✕

Saying Goodbye to the 999 Other Poems

Alan Fox

The following conversation took place 10 March 2003 in Los Angeles. It originally appeared in Rattle *in 2004. Reprinted by permission.*

Fox: Do you remember the first poem you ever wrote?

Lee: Yeah, I guess I do. It was, "Here is a fish, make nice dish," or something like that. I caught a little fish for my mother and I wrote that, I was just learning English, and I was just so amazed that words rhymed.

Fox: So your first poem was in English!

Lee: Right.

Fox: And how do you find writing in English? I assume it's not your first language.

Lee: No, it isn't. It's like my third language. But I keep forgetting languages. My first language is Bahasa Indonesian, and I learned that from my nursemaid. My mother was absent a lot in the beginning because she was trying to get my father out of jail, and so after we left Indonesia I started learning Chinese and I lost all the Bahasa. Then I began to lose a lot of my Chinese when I was about fourteen so English became much more comfortable. I guess it's buried under there. I don't know how that works, Alan. I don't know if you forget it, or it's a buried language.

Fox: It's probably different for different people. I assume you don't use the other languages now, or do you?

Lee: Oh, I do. My mother only speaks Chinese, so I only speak Chinese with her. And I had a brother who recently died, and he didn't speak any English, so I used Chinese with him. But after he died, it dawned on me that the people that I use Chinese with, there's less and less of them. So I feel as if that language, my use of it, is getting less and less.

Fox: Have you written poetry in Chinese?

Lee: No, no, I used to write letters in Chinese to my mother. Up until college, I was still writing letters, but they got more and more elementary and so I don't even write, I can't even read, Chinese any more. But I was back in China about ten years ago, and within a week I was dreaming in Chinese. My wife is Italian-American, and I was answering her in Chinese, so it must have been just natural for me. And I was suddenly able to read a little bit more every day, signs and things, so I think it's under there somewhere probably.

Fox: How is the process of writing poetry for you? Do you write every day, or when you feel like it, or what?

Lee: I don't know, Alan. I feel like I actually am on the job 24 hours a day. I'm always listening for or trying to feel, just to get a sense of that field of mind that you're in when you write, when a poem happens, so I'm always feeling around for that. I'm doing that 24 hours a day, and I'm ready to put everything down to write the poem. I got up this morning about 4:00 because I thought there was something happening. I wanted to sleep in because I went to bed late last night, but I thought, No, no, no, because it doesn't always happen. So I got up and started writing—nothing came of it, a couple of lines. It's so haphazard for me. I don't have a system. I just feel like I'm doing it all the time. It's really inefficient. I've tried to sit down and do it, but it doesn't always work.

Fox: Do you have an idea of what tends to inspire you or the spark that starts the process?

Lee: I don't know, Alan. I've been thinking about it a lot. Lately I've been noticing that any situation I'm in—for instance, this interview—I'm more and more aware that so many things had to happen in order to make this meeting possible. Not only the phone calls and the invitation to the interview and my flying here in the airplane. Somebody had to invent the airplane, right? And then I think, Well, *Rattle* had to have happened for this interview to happen, which means, Stellasue, your life had to have a certain trajectory. Alan, your life had to have a certain trajectory to make all of this happen, right? And I think about the cab driver who took me to the airport and somebody—I just think it's almost too much to disentangle, the myriad things that have to happen to make any situation occur. So I came to the conclusion that everything makes everything happen, and it dawned on me: that's the way a poem happens. So I don't know if there's a particular cause. But a poem somehow is a version of that condition. And I think that's part of the joy of reading poems. When we read a poem, we start to notice how words refer to each other from the beginning of the poem to the end. There's this kind of manifold or myriad field of reference going on, of connections. So I don't know what it is that ever makes me write a poem, you know, the sound of a bird or the smell of leaf mold, my hand, the coffee I had or the coffee I didn't have, or the ache in my left knee. That's part of the frustration because I feel as if at any moment a poem could occur because that condition of *allness*, of *everythingness*, is occurring all the time. And so what is so special about when it yields itself or manifests itself in language? I don't know what that is, but I've been thinking about that. So I guess I don't know what inspires me would be the answer.

Fox: Do you ever have an idea or a wish for what will happen to a poem, how it will be received, or what impact it might have?

Lee: I do. I wish the poem would last forever. I hope that it contributes to the evolution of humanity. That sounds arrogant or claiming too much, doesn't it?

Fox: No, I wouldn't think so, if that's a wish. For me, I would have an idea of where I want it to go, what I want to have happen, perhaps unconsciously.

Lee: And I guess it's happened to me, Alan. Reading poetry has helped me in my own evolving as a human being, so I want to return the favor.

Fox: When you read poetry, what has the greatest impact on you?

Lee: The doorway for me is the emotional: if there's authentic feeling. If there isn't, the poem can be intellectually really wonderful, but I'm not interested. I can appreciate it, I can respect it, I can stand in awe of it even, but if I'm not stirred, I don't take it to my heart.

Fox: And what emotions do you like the best in a poem?

Lee: Maybe it's not even emotions. Maybe what I really love when I read a poem is the visceral experience of a sense of wholeness, that somehow the poem I've encountered is a reflection of a psychic wholeness. It dawns on me, Alan, that every poem is a portrait of a speaker, right? So if my experience of that speaker is a deeply integrated but at the same time a highly differentiated psyche, then I get a real sense of satisfaction, a sense somehow that in the poem the emotional function is well informed of the intellectual function and the intellectual function is informed of the emotional function and they are both informed of the erotic function and the erotic function is informed of the spiritual function. Sometimes I have a problem when I read a poem that's just the mental function; it seems uninformed of the physical functions or the emotional functions or the spiritual functions. Or even a poem that is just the spiritual function working overtime, but uninformed of the other functions. So what I love is a poem that somehow posits, proposes, a condition of wholeness.

Fox: Do you find the emotional part often when you read, or is it rare?

Lee: I think it's very rare. I can't tell, Alan, if it's rare because it's really difficult, or whether for the most part we don't allow it into our lives. It may be disallowed in the culture at large. But maybe we haven't evolved enough. Maybe our emotional function is retarded.

Fox: Maybe poetry is an acceptable way of conveying emotions.

Lee: But then you think about all the poets who we consider great— Eliot or Pound, I don't think they're particularly emotional poets. I see on your shelf there, Yehuda Amachai. I love him because there's a lot of emotion in those poems. That's really rare, and it's emotion that feels to me that it's not uninformed, that it's of his intellect, but the intellect is very informed of the emotions, and they're both informed of their temporality and their eternity. Amachai, I would say, is a poet that really gives me that. But that's rare in English.

Fox: I agree. When we read submissions to *Rattle,* I have one rule: when I read the poem if I'm almost in tears or if I'm laughing, it's in. And that doesn't happen too often, either one.

Lee: Right, right. Why do think that is, Alan?

Fox: I think we look for emotional connection, and I think poetry is a way of doing that.

Lee: But then why are the people who are writing not doing that?

Fox: Ah! I think you've put your finger on it. I think it's tough to do.

Lee: Yes, it's tough to do.

Fox: Do you find that you're inhibited in what you write? Do you ever censor, because you might reveal too much of yourself? Is that an issue for you?

Lee: No. Maybe it is an issue, but it's kind of a backward issue because what I'm trying to do is reveal more and more. And I do recognize that there's something inside of me that resists it. For instance, Stellasue has given me this new strategy into a poem. But there's something that resists being revealed, so for me the problem isn't that I'm revealing too much and I'm trying not to. No, the problem for me is that I'm trying to know myself, to self-reveal, to uncover. In this way poetry is apocalyptic, uncovering, as opposed to ecliptic, covering. And in the same way poetry is disillusioning in the best way—it frees us of our illusions. But there must be something inside of me that resists disillusionment, that wants to hold onto all my illusions, all my narrow definitions of what my self might be.

Fox: What have you written which is successful in conveying emotion in your own work?

Lee: I wrote something just recently that has a lot of emotion in it. I haven't shown it to anybody yet, but I feel like it has a lot of emotion.

Fox: Do you typically show your work to anybody before you send it off for publication?

Lee: I show it to my wife.

Fox: Is she helpful?

Lee: She's very helpful because she has a really good bullshit detector. I just read something to her over the phone. She said, "No, no, no, no, Li-Young, you don't mean that." And I tried to convince her; you know, I'm so defensive. "I did mean it." And she said, "Now think about that. Did you really mean that?" I thought, All right, I didn't mean it. It was just a device or something. She's tough, she doesn't mince any words.

Fox: Is that a good thing for you as a writer?

Lee: I think it is good to have somebody who's not a writer. She comes from a coal-mining background, and she doesn't particularly value literature. But it's also valuable to have fellow poets reading. Which at the moment I don't have.

Fox: It's an interesting issue, the impulse to reveal and yet the contrary impulse to protect.

Lee: I don't know what that's about. It's part of the whole difficulty in writing. When I'm sitting in front of an empty page, part of my problem is I feel like the poem could start anywhere. The page is almost a symbol of pure potential. I could start with the window or the bird or my feet or my shoes or my socks or my nose, my thumb—anywhere. But the minute I put the pencil down on the paper, the minute I start it, then the potential closes down. Then it starts to be about this particular poem. And even though you try to move that poem into a kind of spaciousness, you try to say as much as possible, but even so, it does feel as if you're closing down into this particular poem. And so for me, the experience of writing one poem is saying goodbye to the 999 other poems that want to get written. So sometimes I do have the sense as if I'm like a little doorway and there are 10,000 poems that want to get through. So for me to pick one poem is to say goodbye to 9,999 other poems and that grief just makes me crazy, because I have to pick one. And so sometimes, it doesn't make sense, because what I do is end up closing the door and saying "no" to all of them. The whole thing about revealing is so interesting because I do believe that the practice of poetry is a viable path to self-knowledge. If we study the things that human beings have made, it's a way to study human beings. A poem is a product of the psyche, and it's a way to study the psyche. When we write the poem, we can say,

"Well, here's where I am today." So it's a form of divination. We don't even need to do the I Ching to find out what's going on: we can just write a poem and say, "This is where I am."

Fox: What reward do you get from writing poetry?

Lee: The experience of the *all*. Which is so strange to me because that's our perennial condition. We're always in the *all*. I don't know why we need a piece of art or the writing of poem to remind us. When you're in that trance state, if you're writing the poem, it's almost as if you're omniscient. You know things you didn't know you knew, and you see connections you didn't think were there. And that condition of seeing all those myriad connections at once, it's just that experience of the *all*.

Fox: How would you compare poetry as an art form with other art forms, music or sculpture or painting?

Lee: I think of poetry as a score for the human voice. All art forms reveal us to ourselves so all art forms are viable paths to self-knowledge, to knowledge of our primordial condition, our interconnectedness and interpenetratingness with everything else.

Fox: Do you do many poetry readings?

Lee: I've been doing a lot lately, well, for the last ten years I guess I've been doing a lot.

Fox: Is that something you enjoy?

Lee: I do, I do enjoy it when I remember what it is I would like to do. Because it seems to me that the most a poetry reading can be is the imparting of a kind of inner richness. The worst it can be when the audience feels, Boy, he's really smart, or he's really deep, or he's really interesting. I feel like I've failed. But if I do a reading and the audience goes home and thinks, Wow, inner life is really rich, my inner solitude is really spacious, and maybe as a second or even a third or fourth thought, they think, Hey, he's pretty good, then I succeeded. Again, I'm just returning the favor, because I've gone to readings where that's exactly what I felt after hearing the reading: an inner richness or richness about life, or just being alive, and only almost as an afterthought, that person gave that feeling to me. God bless him, or her. I can't tell whether this is my problem as a listener or the poet's problem when I'm listening, but if I feel, Boy, that person's really smart, or that person really knows how to use language, I feel as if psychic energy has been drained from me but not given back. Then I feel that's not different from TV. I mean, the TV just drains your psychic energy and doesn't give you anything back. In real art, the more psychic energy you put into it, the more you get back. You get it back tenfold.

Fox: Showing off is not helpful, but self-revelation on a deep, true level is.

Lee: That's exactly how I would say it.

Fox: I would think that's one of the most important benefits of poetry, to allow the reader to reveal him- or herself to him- or herself.

Lee: Right. It's a real mysterious and wonderful thing that happens between the reader and the poem.

Fox: Do you find that audiences differ a great deal at your readings?

Lee: They do, in age or gender or class or race, but ultimately I'm trying to hit something that is the same. We're all mortal human beings, part spirit, part matter, dying and eternal, male and female, dark and light, good and bad, so I guess I'm trying not to pay too much attention to the surface quality of the audience. I'm just trying to pay attention to the heart that's afraid, that's jubilant, sad, happy, clapping, singing, grieving. It seems to me that it's all the same heart. It's inflected differently with races and gender, but I never try to tailor the reading, because that could be my downfall, too.

Fox: How do you mean?

Lee: I just read to a high school audience and maybe I walked in there thinking, Well, I don't care, they're 18 or 17 or 16, they're human beings and I'm a human being, so there must be some common ground here, but maybe I was wrong. They were so quiet I thought maybe, Did they all go to sleep, man, or what? Maybe they were just listening well. But maybe I should have tailored it a little more to a 17-year-old, 18-year-old audience. That seems like a bankrupt thing to do, to try to guess your audience. I believe in a common ground.

Fox: Do you ever teach writing?

Lee: I tried it a number of times, just enough times to come to the conclusion I can't do it. It's like sainthood, and I don't even have a little bit of a saint in me. You go in, you open a vein and sometimes the student catches it in a bucket or a cup or a thimble, or they don't catch it at all, and you're bleeding all over the floor. That's what it felt like. It is an incredible service that one is doing, and I wasn't. What am I admitting? That I'm too stingy of spirit to do it? Not everybody is meant to be a teacher, right?

Fox: Absolutely, but look at it from the other point of view: What has helped you the most in terms of learning from others?

Lee: Being around poets helped me a lot. Being around them, seeing how they function in the world. For the most part, I would say how they somehow embody the condition of that "all" in a world that isn't completely friendly to that condition. So the poets that I have always loved, who are living poets that I've loved and been around, their presence has taught me so much about poetry. The way they react to things, the way they see things, they way they are.

Fox: Who are some of your favorite poets?

Lee: I guess ones that come to mind, Gerald Stern, Philip Levine, Galway Kinnell, John Logan, Hayden Carruth, there are so many of them. Emily Dickinson, Robert Frost, Li-po, Tu Fu, Jack Gilbert, Linda Gregg, Michael Palmer, Alan Grossman. There are so many great poets. I think we're living in a really special time. Somebody told me that there are more poets now in North America than there ever has been in the whole world. And I thought, Wow, that's a lot. That's really wonderful.

Fox: Do you find that there are cultural differences in the writing or response to poetry in the United States in comparison with other cultures, other countries?

Lee: I was in Indonesia and I saw this crazy poet. Boy, their idea of a poetry reading was very different. He had an ax hanging from the ceiling, and the ax was swinging back and forth, just missing him. He was ducking and chanting and shouting these poems. And I thought, Wow, that is like nothing I've ever seen. It was an ax head, and it would sometimes stop, and he would swing it again, and it was just swinging around. He was drinking, had a bottle of beer that he broke, and he was lacerating himself with the broken bottle, and chanting poems, and he was in some sort of weird trance. I couldn't tell whether it was theatrics or real, but the other people seemed in this trance with him. They were really into it, and shouting, and clapping, and responding gutturally, grunting when he was. But there must be some sort of cultural background for that, right? If we did that in this country, it would be just sensationalism?

Fox: Probably.

Lee: I've noticed in Indonesia the possessed quality of poetry had not gone out of favor yet. In North America or in Eurocentric countries we are suspicious of somebody who believes that poetry is a form of possession by higher powers.

Fox: Do you think that over the past 20 or 30 or 40 years poetry in the United States has become more popular, less popular?

Lee: More popular. There are more poets writing, more books published, more magazines, more MFA programs. The downside could be when we forget that it's ultimately about spirit. The upside would be it's a sign of our evolution.

Fox: Do you think that the writing of poetry can be taught?

Lee: I hope so. I feel as if I'm teaching myself. Maybe, not taught from the outside. It can be taught as a road to the interior. It can be taught that way, but I don't think it can be taught like this writing scheme or this meter, or something like that.

Fox: What suggestions do you have for a new poetry writer?

Lee: Boy, I feel like a new poetry writer, Alan. Just keep doing it, believe in yourself, remind yourself. It's the deepest thing you're probably doing. Well, that's not true: there are deeper things, such as raising children. Just keep believing in what you're doing.

Fox: Do you like to hang out with poets?

Lee: I do. Some of the poets I mentioned, I love being in their presence. They always teach me to be more expansive, more welcoming, more accepting, compassionate. Maybe I've been lucky because I've heard poets are terrible, they're stingy and self-aggrandizing, but that hasn't been my experience. The poets I've known have all been extremely capacious in their emotional range, in their acceptance, in what they love and what they'll tolerate. Maybe I'm just lucky. I don't get to be around them all the time because of my conditions of work and family and where I'm at. There aren't that many in Chicago.

Fox: You mentioned compassion. What's the role of compassion in poetry?

Lee: I'm almost embarrassed to talk about this stuff because it's so murky. If it weren't for poetry I would be a worse human being. I can remember the day when I discovered the idea of writing poetry. I started to think, Wait a minute, I have to change. In order to write these poems I love so much, in order to write like, for instance, Emily Dickinson, I have to change. What she's doing isn't a technical issue at all; it's about her being. And for me to write like that, I would have to get to that place, that complete openness and self-acceptance and self-forgiveness. I know there's a lot of pain in those poems, but she's willing to forgive what she's doing in those poems, that is, be irrational, defy probability, all that stuff. I thought, OK, how do I reach that place in order to write like that? In order to earn the authority to say that? So I thought, I have to change.

Fox: Wonderful insight. So what did you do when you had this realization?

Lee: I just started thinking about why. It made me more self-reflective, noticing how I'm not consistent with what it is I'm saying. The poems somehow live ahead of me because they're a paradigm for what I want to be, a paradigm for the consciousness or the love or the compassion or the tenderness that I want to embody. If I read Roethke with the tenderness he has for the natural world, I would have to ask myself, How do I get to that place, to be that tender? Or John Logan. I was just reading his poems, and I know a lot of people think he's sentimental and overwrought, but I don't. He's tender and a master of the line. I just ask myself, How do I get to that place, to be able to say those things with authority? And I don't know how. I guess maybe making the poem is self-making. Yeats said about revising poems: "It is myself I'm making."

Fox: I think that to be a really good writer you have to access yourself in a true way.

Lee: Yes. I think ultimately, Alan, what I've been trying to say so clumsily for this past hour is I don't think the poem or the poetry is the final opus. I don't think the work is the poem or book of poems or the novel or the painting. It's the self and that the making of the art is a way toward that total presence that one is trying to achieve. You can't just go through the world and try to be. I think art is a viable path toward total presence.

Fox: Yes.

Lee: That took, what, three seconds to say. I should have said it in the beginning. The total presence is the grail. The poem is not the grail. The poem is a kind of divination. You write a poem, and you look at it and you go, Wow, I'm really dark today. And you say, Why? That's a really incomplete, unfair view of existence. And then you realize you have to work through something. I look at the poem as looking into the mirror. How do I look today? How does my soul look today? But then, of course, you have to have some sort of ideal as to what a poem that manifests total presence would look like. And I think we do have models of that.

Fox: Such as?

Lee: I would say certain great poems by Robert Frost, like "Directive," "West-Running Brook"—boy, that poem just breaks my heart every time I read it. That poem, "West-Running Brook," is just amazing. The need of being versed in country things, poems like that, that give you an experience of total presence. Or even in Neruda's poems, in *Residence on Earth,* even in their translations, somehow the presence gets translated. The work is not even the poem; the work is the self.

Fox: Poetry is—you used a good word—the mysterious.

Lee: It really is.

Fox: The process, the result, it's very mysterious. I think it calls upon the poet to really look at himself or herself.

Lee: Yes, and it's ultimately a kind of alchemy, Alan. Even a metaphor. We could think of it as a literary device, but that's just so bankrupt to me, it just feels nauseating to me. But ultimately a metaphor marries two seemingly incompatible psychic contents. It marries them in an image that's a metaphor, so it's alchemical, right? You're trying to happily integrate parts of your psyche that resist integration, maybe it's feeling and thinking, but then you find an image, and image is like a perfect marriage of thinking and feeling. Whereas a statement would be all thinking. But an image or a metaphor is that composite of thinking, feeling, everything married together.

Fox: Why do you write poetry instead of novels or short stories or something else?

Lee: I have this theory, Alan. I notice, for instance, a poem is the scored human voice. Voice is speech, and all speech is done with the exhaled breath. You can't inhale and speak so you have to breathe out. Unfortunately, or fortunately, the exhaled breath is the dying breath. When we breathe in, our bodies are full of life, our muscles have real tone, our blood is full of oxygen, our bones actually get very compacted, they actually get harder. There's some proof for this, and we feel full of life and very comfortable. And when we exhale, our bones get softer, our muscles lose their tone and it's the dying breath. Now when we speak, we're using that dying breath. I think that gives writing a particularly *tragic color*, because you're using the dying breath, inflecting or figuring your dying breath. But meaning gets born. The more you speak, the more meaning gets revealed so that meaning grows in opposite ratio to the vitality of the dying breath. As meaning gets bigger, the breath gets less and less. Which seems to me a paradigm of life—that as we die the meaning of our lives gets born, and that seems tragic to me. Because one feels so sharply that one is engaging in one's own dying, when you're scoring the human speech, you try to ransom that breath, you try to make it count as much as possible by packing it with as much psychic content as possible. The language that most approaches that state is poetry. A sentence of poetry is more packed than any other form of speech with psychic content, emotional content, intellectual content, spiritual content, visceral content. You're more aware you have to spend this breath to give birth to meaning. Robert Frost knew that. He said,

"Well spent is kept." To keep the meaning you have to spend the breath.

Fox: I think what you're doing now is like the process of writing a poem.

Lee: I'm also thinking there's all these weird trajectories of force that go on when we write a sentence of speech. While vitality decreases, meaning gets born, and yet potential decreases. The beginning of the line is pure potential. Before you even put a word down you're in a state of pure potential, but as the line proceeds, the potential is closed down. But then the poem keeps bringing your hand or your thinking back to the beginning of the line so it enacts this desire to return to pure potential all the time. You're actually enacting in the writing of a poem the deepest laws that govern the universe. I don't know why that should be a surprise, because ultimately if a poem is a paradigm of psyche and if psyche is a paradigm of cosmos, then, it's obvious that a poem would be a paradigm of the all. Why is it every time I think about it it seems surprising or novel? You're trying to ransom that dying breath. You just can't stand the thought of death, so you try to pack everything in as much as possible.

Fox: Is that why many people have an aversion to poetry?

Lee: Yes! Of course! They can't stand that density, the total presence. It is too much. Why is it too much?

Fox: Ah.

Lee: I think this is a weird time we're living in, Alan, because I've noticed, for instance, people's reactions to certain words. We're living in a time where the word *sincere* is suddenly a bad thing. I don't get it. I heard a poet say to me, "Oh, I hate sincerity." And I thought, Oh, what do you like? Insincerity? I was talking to a poet and I said to her, "Well, for me, poetry as a form is disillusionment, right? It frees you of your illusions in order to uncover the condition of the all which we are constantly in the midst of." And she said, 'Well, I don't like to be disillusioned.' "Why? You want to be illusioned?" Hollywood gives us illusions. *People Magazine* gives us illusions. TV gives us illusions. But I think art gives us reality. And the reality that's uncovered is so rich. Maybe that's what it is—it's not only rich and beautiful but it's terrifying, too. Because it's so limitless it's overwhelming. We can't stand abundance and so we keep making models of scarcity. Horizontal models are all based on scarcity, but vertical models are based on abundance. We can't stand the fact that ultimately this condition of the *allness* is what is our real condition. And so we don't want to be disillusioned. I want to be disillusioned. When I first read the poets that I love, I thought, Wow, you mean, this is real existence, this is somebody speaking truthfully about my own experience of the *all?* And I just don't want to live in illusion. And yet I'm my own worst enemy. I do recognize that I keep creating little illusions I can function inside of.

Fox: How would you say your work has evolved in the past ten or twenty years?

Lee: Well, I hope it's gotten better, deeper, truer.

Fox: What would you consider to be better?

Lee: Fuller, fuller, more—the word that comes to mind is—*naked,* less, less dressing, more the thing, the true speaking directly, what it is, is exactly my experience, less dressing, fuller, more differentiated and at the same time integrating more psychic contents. I hope the presence that those poems impart is fuller, deeper.

Fox: And what would you like your work to be remembered for?

Lee: Oh, man, I don't know. I just want to write a good poem.

Finding a Voice for the Condition of Allness

Earl G. Ingersoll

The following conversation took place 19 November 2004 in a crowded, and noisy, restaurant in the East Village of New York City. Also participating is Lee's editor Thom Ward, the editor of BOA Editions, Ltd., Lee's publisher.

><del>~~~</del><

Ingersoll: I'd like to begin by asking you how you feel about being interviewed. One of the things that amazed me, once I got started with this project, was how many interviews you've been involved in— 25 or 30 interviews, which is quite a few for somebody who's not 89. I'm curious how you feel when someone turns on the tape recorder: Are you anxious? Do you dread it?

Lee: I guess all of that. I'm anxious, I'm excited, I dread it. But it's fascinating for me, too, because we talk about poetry during most of the interviews so it's language about language, and I find it a happy thing to be thinking out loud about language, about words, about literature.

Ingersoll: Do you get anxious that these words you're speaking now, for example, become the property of this machine and then me as your interviewer so they're out of your control. Does that bother you?

Lee: No, that's part of the pleasure, in a way. I mean, as long as what I'm saying isn't completely distorted and as long as it's taken within a certain context or a historical moment. It can be very exciting to be in the unknown.

Ingersoll: So it's a kind of exploration of the unknown with somebody.

Lee: It can be the practice of a certain kind of presence. I almost feel as if what we're doing is being present to our own minds in a way we wouldn't normally be.

Ingersoll: Have you ever felt that everybody is asking the same question?

Lee: In the beginning there were a lot of questions about my biography, and now I've resisted talking about that so much.

Ingersoll: Your ethnicity and origins?

Lee: For a while there, that was the primary topic. I lost interest.

Ingersoll: One of the things that interested me in your responses was that I got the sense people were trying to pin you down as "Asian-American." They wanted to push you into that pigeonhole, and you were resisting that, and saying, "I'm an American poet. I don't think of myself as an Asian-American poet."

Lee: You know, I don't know whether that was such a good thing to do. I have friends who write about ethnicity and race, and they're very angry with me. They say that somehow I don't own up to my Asian identity, and part of me says, "But I do it on a day-to-day basis. I do it everyday with my life." But as an artist I'm trying to get in touch with something that can't be accounted for by my gender, my race, my ethnicity, my class, my historical moment. Those all figure into it. But the math isn't what we think it is. It isn't like, Oh, you're this gender, you're this race, so you should write this kind of poetry. Poems are unaccountable. They're not accountable by only race or gender or whatever. And you can't account for my personal life only by those specifications.

I'm interested in the nature of reality, and I don't think constantly wondering about my ethnicity can lead me to a firmer grasp of the nature of reality. I think it can up to a point; for instance, I think it's a very important thing to think about racism in terms of projection and transference. It's important to recognize that, but it seems to me that after we recognize that, then there's real work to be done, withdrawing your projections. I think poetry for me is ultimately a mode of withdrawn projection. Is that possible?

Ward: I think so. One of the concerns I see in your poetry after reading and editing it is the interplay between language and silence.

The other morning when I woke up my nine-year-old, the first thing he said was, "You know, Dad, an echo is a shadow of sound." I thought, That's something my friend Li-Young Lee would like to wrestle with.

We all know how important the Bible has been to you. What other books you've read, past or recent, have come back to haunt you, in the best sense of the word *haunt?* What are some of the books that have unconsciously empowered you in your writing?

Lee: You know, my reading is very—what is the word?—desultory. I'm not very disciplined; I just read all over the place. You know, the one I keep going back to is Meister Eckhart. It's not even the concepts *per se*; it's the way he thinks. Right now I'm reading Nietzsche again, and Nietzsche's making a lot more sense this time round. I don't know why. When I was younger, I said, "I don't like this cult of the strong." But I don't see it that way recently. I've been reading *Thus Spake Zarathustra.* It's such a beautiful book, so tragic.

Ward: And there's a lot about the empowerment of the artist and the poet as creator in there, too.

Lee: You know, I've been thinking, It's the bonds between letters that create words, and it's the bonds between words that create sentences. And those bonds can be dissolved—what would be the opposite of *binding?*

Ward: . . . *rending.*

Lee: Yes, *rending.* So poetry could be a way to create new bonds and even to rend meanings so that new meanings can enter.

Ingersoll: Actually you have a favorite word from your own poetry—*cleaving*—which can mean both "binding" and "rending." It's a wonderful word with its opposing meanings.

Lee: Yes, maybe that's what I was thinking about.

Ingersoll: To follow up on Thom's question, any other book that "haunts" you?

Lee: *Grimm's Fairy-Tales* and Italian folk tales, especially those by Italo Calvino. Italian folk tales are beautiful, but I find them very repetitive. In *Grimm's Fairy-Tales* there's a lot more variation, and yet they maintain their archetypal significance. The patterns are reconfigured in more various and interesting ways.

Ward: You also read philosophy, like Heidegger, don't you?

Lee: But I've sworn off philosophy because I think it's flawed somehow. Lately, every time I read even a few pages of a philosopher I think, Just get to it! The answer's poetry. The conclusions philosophers keep arriving at are just various ways to say the same thing. And the same thing is that the practice of poetic being or aesthetic being in the world is a value. It's a value-creating mode of being. That's what it comes down to—all that stuff with Heidegger. He spends pages talking about what is thinking, like three pages talking about a door closing and listening to it, and he's trying to decide whether he heard it first and blah, blah, blah, and I think, the answer to your problem is aesthetic presence. It seems to me he suffers from a malaise, or a malady, an illness of the philosophical mind.

Ingersoll: I'd like to take you back to the Bible because that's been one of the enduring elements in your interviews. In our conversation before the interview began, you were talking about your more recent views of the Bible and posing the question about the father-son relationship and . . .

Lee: You know, Earl, I'm so troubled by that book. About a month ago I was rereading the Book of Luke, where Jesus says, "I *am* the son of God. I *am* the way." You know, If you've seen me, you've seen the way, and I thought, If somebody sat across from me in a chair and said that, I'd say, "That's proof you are not."

Ward: You mean, There's only one way to the Father, and that's through Me.

Lee: I would say that's proof you're not the Way. Because nobody who *knows* would say that. Then, I thought, OK, so what words in the Gospel were the words that *really* made sense to me. Then I thought that the Gospels can be separated into two things: one where Christ's saying things like the Beatitudes, where He's saying real metaphysical truths, and then there's the other stuff which seems to me the worst of spiritual seeking. I mean, the best of spiritual seeking is in there, too. They're both in there. That puzzles me.

    And I was thinking about the Jewish tradition of the *midrash*. Do you know that? That's the retelling of stories from the Torah and letting your imagination work in the retelling so you're also improvising a little. And your improvisations reveal something about yourself. And I realized we do that naturally. We think about something, and it changes in our memory. And even the way we change it tells us something about the reality we've created.

Ingersoll: So every retelling is a kind of rewriting of the tale. Suppose, Li-Young, you were retelling the story of Abraham and Isaac we were talking about earlier. What's your take on that story?

Lee: You know, sacrifice is a big issue for me. I don't know who said it, but you can't sacrifice something lesser for something greater. That's not a sacrifice. It's just trying to get something greater for something less. Then I think, What was the nature of the sacrifices that keep occurring in the Bible? And what is this repetition of the slaughter of the son? What is that about, ultimately? Isaac. Joseph gets thrown into the well, although he gets that done by his brothers, but there again the son was threatened. And then of course there's Jesus. And I think, What is this myth about, this slaughter of the son? And there's Absalom. I keep thinking there's a struggle between the actual presence of father and son in the Bible, literally. Abraham is a father figure. He's very large in the Old Testament. The Isaac figure somehow doesn't have as much potency. Now this is *my* imagination. Now Isaac's children were . . . Jacob and Esau? What's interesting to me is that in the Jacob and Esau story the sons are the main characters. They're in the foreground. In the Abraham and Isaac story the father was in the foreground. Isaac was the sacrificial victim.

Ward: I don't think Isaac speaks in the Abraham and Isaac story.

Ingersoll: When they get to the sacrificial altar doesn't he ask Abraham where the sacrificial lamb is?

Ward: Correct.

Lee: I have a theory about that. The Bible says there's a ram stuck in the thicket. This is the *midrash* thing, and I'm wondering why my imagination is going in this direction. The Bible says there was a ram stuck in the thicket, but I don't think it was a ram. I think it was some boy, like a slave boy, but that's too heinous a story, because where's the sacrifice if it's just a ram. That's number one. Number two, there's this weird substitution that goes on when Jacob robs Esau of his legacy. The mother puts a cloak over Jacob and he goes in, and the father, Isaac, thinks it's Esau, the brother. Now I'm wondering, Did the mother of Isaac do that with Abraham? The Bible does say that on the morning they were leaving to go up onto the mountain the mother was standing at the tent, watching them, and I remember thinking, Why did they mention that? That's such a moving and terrifying thing—to have her watching it. I mean, when you think of it, if I get up at five o'clock in the morning and wrap a big butcher knife up in a piece of cloth and take my son off with me, I'd be psychotic. Right? And my wife is standing in the doorway watching us go. She's beginning to figure it out.

Ingersoll: But isn't it partly too that Isaac represents a miracle, that he came as this almost divine gift to this old couple who'd long before given up the hope of having a child and to sacrifice that child makes it an even greater sacrifice?

Lee: But here's the thing, though: it isn't a sacrifice if it's for something higher. What was the higher good?

Ward: An allegiance to God? We're moving toward Job country here. I mean, talk about sacrifice! Nobody sacrificed more than Job—his children, his servants, and all his livestock. He goes from Donald Trump to Skid Row in a heartbeat.

Ingersoll: I've always had trouble with that story, and with the system that says, OK, you've passed the test; now you get it all back. How would you deal with the replacement kids? I'm with you, Li-Young, these are tough stories.

Lee: Now, here's the thing: what if every little thing gets restored to Job? What if there really is literally the reincarnation, every 400,000 years? I mean, every 400,000 years we're back here?

Ward: I'm bumming out about that. I want one and out, Baby. I wake up every morning and say, Oh shit, I'm still me. I want this to be the threshold to something else, not return here as the angel-beast I am, with all my ambiguities and ambivalences. No, I definitely don't want that. I become more and more fascinated with the beforeness, what was before the chromosome, the 46 that I am supposedly. Is it a circle back to the Apple or are we really stuck in some linear deal, diachronic time? Or is there synchronic un-time? These are concerns of your work, the issues that inform your poetry.

Lee: I love thinking about this stuff, but we haven't been talking about anything pertinent.

Ingersoll: I want to circle back to the metaphor that's here in the title of your latest collection of poems, *Book of My Nights*. Do you do *all* of your work at night, all of the drafting, revising, etc.

Lee: In that book I did. And I work almost completely at night.

Ingersoll: Could you conceive of being switched to the "day shift"?

Lee: No, I would get depressed. Evenings are great. I know what to do in the evening. There is this weird time of day, and I think, What is this time of day about? Maybe between 1:30 and 3:30 in the afternoon. I think, What am I supposed to do with this? And I get depressed.

Ingersoll: I ask in part because you make such a point of access to the inner voice, and I'm wondering if night time is the best time to get in touch with that inner voice.

Lee: Yes, it is for me. It's almost a cliché. I've always felt funny about it because it always means it's the last voice. And maybe there are writers for whom it's the first voice. Stafford wrote in the morning. Maybe there are two kinds of poetic utterance. The utterance of the *puer*, in Latin "boy," and the utterance of the *senex*, the "old man." There are two kinds of wisdom, and they're both in touch with the source. In the case of the "*puer*" he's in touch with the source because he's so recently broken away from it. In the case of the "*senex*" he's in touch with the source because of his mortality. In the first case it would be the language of poetic utterance before experience. It's the voice, in a way, of innocence. And then there's the voice after experience, the voice of the "*senex*," that is, a voice that's come to wisdom, that's processed experience.

Ward: Some of us who are morning writers can't write at midnight because of that great void of complete silence. In the morning as I write I can hear the birds, or maybe a garbage truck. How do you deal with that pure silence at night?

Lee: You know, it's not pure silence in the city.

Ward: Well, I live out in the country—suburbs, where, especially in the winter, there's not a sound at night.

Lee: I'm guessing I would love that because I do remember that as a child living in a little town. I loved that.

But you know, I've been hiding all my life, hiding from my parents, right? And my parents were hiding from the authorities so there's this issue of hiding. Maybe that's why I write at night. I don't mean to imply that writers who write in the morning necessarily write as children. I'm just wondering about these two threshold states.

Ward: There's the wisdom of the child, that you can't say is of the depth of the wisdom of the older person, but there's always this relationship. I remember my child at three asking how old his g. p., or Grandpa, was, and when I told him that Grandpa was 66, he said, "You know what? He's old. And you know what? I'm new."

Lee: Frost has a wonderful poem, "West-Running Brook," in which the woman says, "Are we old, or are we new?"

Ingersoll: Thom tells me you're putting together a new collection of poems. How does that go? One, how do you know it's time to? Two, how do you feel about doing it? I mean, are you saying goodbye to those poems in a way? How do you do it? Do you have some special way of organizing, selecting the poems?

Lee: I think for each book it was different. In this particular instance, I think the reason we're going to put together some poems is that I've been going on readings and a lot of people have been saying, "Can I have a copy of that poem you just read? Is it in any of your books." I've been saying, "If you give me a stamped, self-addressed envelope I'll mail it to you." I think I've mailed hundreds of copies of these poems. I'm thinking, Maybe people like them, and they're ready to be published. I'm mailing them out for free; maybe I should put them in a book. Not just to sell them, but maybe they're ready to be in a book. In this case that's how this book evolved. In the last one I think it was different. I think Thom was saying, "It's time!" In each instance there was a different impetus pushing the book out into the world.

Ingersoll: But you have to decide what goes in and what doesn't go in. How does that work?

Lee: I just try to pick what I think are the best poems and run them past Thom. Poems that are inventive enough, and interesting enough, and where there's enough imagination.

Ingersoll: Now does Thom say, "Instead of that one why don't you include this one"?

Lee: Yeah, I guess he does.

Ward: One of the things I did in the last book was with a poem I didn't think was going where it could, and you made two poems out of it. If there was one thing I learned from Al [Poulin, the founder of BOA Editions] it's how to help writers in their own terms. The way I work with Li-Young is different from the way I work with Lucille [Clifton] or [W. D.] Snodgrass. I try to offer the poet, let's say, a line or a stanza, and we'll call it "A." And the poet will have in his or her mind "B" and might say, "You know, maybe you're right. I didn't feel comfortable with that line or image." My happy job is to say, "Think about my 'A' and your 'B' when you revise, and like with the Hegelian dialectic—'Q' or 'J' will arise. It won't be my 'A' or your 'B,' but those forces will unconsciously empower a new revelatory or apocalyptic moment." I don't feel my job as editor is to prescribe, but to suggest, to open the doors of perception, but it's the poet's task to make a decision to walk through.

Ingersoll: I'm wondering, Li-Young, what effect it has on you in doing the organizing of poems into a book. I'm thinking of these block-buster exhibits at the Met, like the two van Gogh shows back in the '80s. Some people got tremendously excited by seeing for the first time two paintings of the same subject next to each other on the wall. Does that happen to you as you put two poems next to each other in the manuscript?

Lee: Yeah, it does. Sometimes it creates a good effect, and sometimes it's bad. Sometimes I put the poems together, and I think, Wow, I guess my inner life was OK during this time because there's a lot of richness there. Sometimes I put a certain bunch of poems together, and I think, That's *terrible*. My inner life seemed really thick and monotonous. Because I write as a form of divination. I write the poem to see how I am. Even if the poem has suffering, but if it's full of invention, if I'm making moves with my heart and my mind and my soul that are lively and full of richness and possibility, then I feel, Well, I must be still alive. You know, I'm making a lot of vivid, vital moves intellectually and emotionally on the page. But if I write a poem and it comes out very flat on the page, then I think, Why am I writing like this? Then if I put the poems all together, and I see certain consistencies, I'm always amazed. Even with *Book of My Nights* I was surprised that all those poems had so much night in them. I didn't set out to write them that way.

Ingersoll: The reason I'm asking is that I've heard other poets say that this can be a very revealing activity. They might say, No, this poem doesn't belong here. Or, this one belongs next to that one. Do you do that? I should think that would be very exciting.

Lee: Yes, I do that. It is exciting. It's like composing the stanzas of a poem.

Ingersoll: Your speaking about sending out poems to people who asked for them after your readings opens the door to the question of your sense of audience.

Lee: I think the narrative-lyric mode is basically one in which the audience is behind a curtain so the dialogue is with your own divinity, and the audience overhears it. When you're reading a poem, the feeling is always that you're overhearing somebody speak to himself, which is some bigger part of himself, or to some totality of himself, or herself, or to God. So what we're actually witnessing, for instance, in Lorca is his wrestling with *duende* and Emily Dickinson is wrestling with God and mortality, with Whitman it's God and America, but it's always an *other* thing—America, God, mortality, *duende*. It's always some demon, *daimon*, divine figure. It's a triaxial state of affairs: you have the poet, the poet's demon, and the audience as witness. I think it's only seldom that they're actually addressed. I think it's very seldom that I'm actually writing *to* an audience. I'm usually enacting my own demon.

Ingersoll: In working with the interviews, I've shared with so many people the story of Li-po finishing a poem, folding it in the shape of a boat, and sailing it down a nearby stream. It seems so liberating to me as a writer to be free of the concern with the end-product of writing, to remind myself it's the process, the moment of the creating that finally matters.

Ward: And there are those Tibetan monks who make mandalas out of colored sand and when they're done they go and dump them into the river. Most Americans are completely frazzled by such an action. The Western mind is all ends oriented, not process oriented.

Lee: Well, here's the other thing, too. A lot of that comes from us not recognizing what the Grail is. For instance, some might look at that sand painting and think, The Grail is the sand painting. Or I might think, This poem I've written on this page is the Grail. That's because we don't trust the possibility that after having written the poem you're changed on a cellular level, and I think repeatedly doing that with your mind it really changes you physically.

We were talking earlier about the Bible, and I think it's written in a certain way that if I can just turn my head the right way I can see the way all the plates are lining up, and I can say, "Oh!" then my vision of the world would change. I would not walk through the world with blinders on anymore. I would suddenly see the deeper paradigms that are being disclosed, the deeper orders. Sometimes I think the practice of reading literature must change us on a cellular level, so after those monks have done that painting they're *changed.* If we had different glasses on we could see that their body structures have changed. Their cells are different. And the sand painting, what's that?! We don't know what the Grail is.

Ingersoll: On the subject of the poet seeking the true Grail, we were talking earlier about your sons, and I'd like to pose this hypothetical situation: suppose one of your sons came to you and said he wanted to become a poet. What would you tell him he needed to do to prepare for becoming a poet? Or, what do you see as the apprenticeship of a poet?

Lee: I don't know, Earl. I know this sounds crazy, but if my son said to me, "I want to become a poet" it would be as if he were saying, "I want to marry God." Part of me feels, Yay! Part of me wants to say, "Why would you want to do that? Why would you want to marry God?"

I feel that when a person writes poems they're trying to hear a voice, or construct a voice, or discover a voice, or uncover a voice, that is not human, that includes the human, but is beyond the human, deeper than the human, older than the human. It is the voice that is prior to the human. The source of language and the source of reality are the same in a poem. It's like the ancient poets saying, "Sing, muses." It's like saying, "Sing, gods." They're bigger than we are, and older. You know, they're *daimons*, demons. I think the mission of poetry is to impart a divinized voice. Otherwise, all we would have is language as it exists in its social spectrum, i.e., language is important there as a conveyance of information and social representations. But I think divinized language is why poetry is important. There's no way to divinize language except to open oneself up to deep, unconscious influences, to integrate deep, deep, and sometime massive amounts of psychic material. And even transpsychic material.

    I feel my work as a poet is to come to terms with not only my personal history but also my species history so that my work has to be specific not only to me but to my species. I know it may sound crazy, but it's like having the universe speak to you. I feel that anything we look at, anything at all, this tape recorder, is part of a larger order. If we examine how this tape recorder came to be here, we'd have to, first of all, account for you because you brought it into this restaurant. Then we'd have to account for the inventor of the tape recorder. If you flew here, we'd have to account for the pilot, and so on. So if we look at any specific thing in the world, everything and anything resides in a center of what I call a totality of causes. I mean, it's such a finely, myriadly woven net of cause and effect that brought this tape recorder to this table. It's expedient to say that you brought it. But in fact everything exists in the middle of this totality of causes, and I feel that that condition of allness, if it had a voice, that voice would be poetry. Poetry is basically the locally inflected voice of the condition of allness. That condition of allness, it seems to me, is God. I mean, if I sat here, completely aware of the myriad of circumstances in this finely woven net of causes that have brought me to the position of sitting here at this moment—all the food I ate, my parents, how we set this meeting up, the telephones involved—what a net of circumstances!

Ingersoll: It sounds to me, and I know very little about it, but it sounds like what's popularly known as "chaos theory," where the fluttering of a butterfly's wings in the Amazon rainforest can lead to a hurricane in the Bahamas—that sense of everything being connected.

Lee: I don't understand that, Earl! How is that "chaos"? It sounds like "order" to me. *Chaos* would imply that nothing's connected. But it seems to me that that condition of allness—and we know that by what they call six degrees of separation, that you're connected to anybody else in the world by six steps—so what would it sound like if somebody suddenly opened up his mind to that condition that we are constantly living in? That would be poetry. Because a poem, it seems to me, is basically a remote instance of that condition, and in a good one there are connections being made throughout the poem that you can't even foresee, connections to other images and other references so in the poem itself there is a spherical condition of infinitely referenced elements.

Ingersoll: So the poem is a kind of replica of that allness you were speaking of.

Lee: Yes. If my son said, "I'm going to practice the condition of allness and write from that perspective," I would say, "God bless you!" at the same time I would say, "Oh no." I know what happened to William Blake. That's what I meant when I said that my son announcing he wanted to become a poet would be like his saying he wanted to marry God, to be marrying that allness, to be examining, meditating about that condition of allness all the time.

><⁓><⁓><

About the Author

Li-Young Lee was born of Chinese parents in Jakarta, Indonesia. His family moved to the United States in 1964. Mr. Lee lives in Chicago with his wife and two sons. He is the author of three books of poetry: *Rose, The City in Which I Love You,* and *Book of My Nights,* all published by BOA Editions. *Rose* received the Delmore Schwartz Award, *The City in Which I Love You* was the 1990 Lamont Poetry Selection of The Academy of American Poets, and *Book of My Nights* was the winner of the Poetry Society of America's 2002 William Carlos Williams Award. Mr. Lee is also the author of the memoir *The Winged Seed.*

About the Editor

Earl G. Ingersoll is a Distinguished Professor Emeritus at the State University of New York, College at Brockport. He is the author or editor of eleven books, including collections of interviews with Margaret Atwood, Lawrence Durrell, Doris Lessing, and, most recently, Rita Dove.

Index

A

Abraham *39, 176*
Absalom *22, 176*
AIDS *62*
Amachai, Yehuda *160*
Angelou, Maya *72*

B

Berryman, John *82*
Betrayal of Images (Magritte) *150*
Beuys, Joseph *26*
Bible, The *11, 19, 22, 26, 30, 36, 59, 95, 149, 176–77, 182*; Book of Acts, *107*; Book of Exodus, *32, 39, 76–77*; Book of Luke, *175*; Ecclesiastes, *39, 42*; Epistles, The, *128*; Gospel of John, *150*; Proverbs, *32*; Psalms, *32, 33, 76*; Song of Songs, *39, 42. See also individual names.*
Blake, William *75, 98, 144, 154, 184*
Buddhism *118–119*

C

Calvino, Italo *174*
Cantos, The (Pound) *125*
Carruth, Hayden *165*
Cavafy, C. P. *150*
Char, René *107*
Chin, Frank *95*
China *9, 19–20, 30, 38–39*
Clifton, Lucille *180*
Crane, Hart *86, 88*
Cultural Revolution *9, 30*

D

Dante *75, 127*
David, King *23, 42, 127, 135, 142*
Delilah *22*
Dickinson, Emily *10, 11, 12, 14, 62, 64, 75, 77, 96, 106, 115, 122, 146, 154, 165, 167, 181*
Donne, John *46, 125, 127*

E

Eckhart, Johannes. *See* Meister Eckhart
Eliot, T. S. *74, 81, 117, 118, 125, 127, 128, 135, 160*; *Four Quartets, 126*; *The Waste Land, 125–26*
Emerson, Ralph Waldo *21, 28, 75, 77–78, 96*
Esau *176*

F

Faulkner, William *83, 110*; *As I Lay Dying, 83, 90, 110, 121*; "The Bear," *83, 90*; *The Sound and the Fury, 83*
Frost, Robert *63, 81, 96, 137, 144, 165, 169–70*; "Birches," *77*; "Directive," *95, 128, 168*; "West-Running Brook," *168, 179*

G

Gilbert, Jack *165*

Boa Editions, Ltd.
American Reader Series

No. 1   *Christmas at the Four Corners of the Earth*
Prose by Blaise Cendrars
Translated by Bertrand Mathieu

No. 2   *Pig Notes & Dumb Music: Prose on Poetry*
By William Heyen

No. 3   *After-Images: Autobiographical Sketches*
By W. D. Snodgrass

No. 4   *Walking Light: Memoirs and Essays on Poetry*
By Stephen Dunn

No. 5   *To Sound Like Yourself: Essays on Poetry*
By W. D. Snodgrass

No. 6   *You Alone Are Real to Me: Remembering Rainer Maria Rilke*
By Lou Andreas-Salomé

No. 7   *Breaking the Alabaster Jar: Conversations with Li-Young Lee*
Edited by Earl G. Ingersoll

Colophon

*Breaking the Alabaster Jar: Conversations with
Li-Young Lee* was typeset by Richard Foerster,
York Beach, Maine, using New Baskerville and
Parisian fonts. The cover was designed by Lisa
Mauro with a photo by Andrew Downes. The
back cover artwork, "Symbiology," is by Li-Lin
Lee; the photo is courtesy of Walsh Gallery.
Manufacturing is by McNaughton & Gunn,
Saline, Michigan.

>···~···<

The publication of this book was made possible,
in part, by the special support of the following
individuals:

Alan & Nancy Cameros ❖ Gwen & Gary
Conners ❖ Burch & Louise Craig ❖ Susan S.
Feinstein ❖ Bev & Pete French ❖ Andy
& Jacquie Germanow ❖ Dane & Judy Gordon
❖ Gerard & Suzanne Gouvernet ❖ Kip & Deb
Hale ❖ William B. Hauser ❖ Peter & Robin
Hursh ❖ Robert & Willy Hursh ❖ Earl G.
Ingersoll ❖ Bill Johnson & Susie Cohen
❖ Archie & Pat Kutz ❖ Rosemary & Lew
Lloyd ❖ Ruth & Irving Malin ❖ Richard
Margolis & Sherry Phillips ❖ Robert & Frances
Marx ❖ Jeffrey Metzger & Robin Hamilton
❖ Daniel M. Meyers ❖ Jimmy & Wendy
Mnookin ❖ Suzanne Nelson ❖ Boo Poulin
❖ Thom Satterlee ❖ Jane M. Schuster ❖ Sue
S. Stewart ❖ Thomas R. Ward ❖ Pat & Michael
Wilder ❖ Geraldine Zetzel

>···~···<